World War Two

An illustrated
History in colour
1939-1945

Robert Hoare
Edited by R J Unstead

Special Adviser:
Dr J M Roberts
Fellow and Tutor in Modern History
at Merton College, Oxford

Macdonald Educational

© 1973 Macdonald and Company
(Publishers) Limited
49-50 Poland Street
London W I A 2LG

SBN 356 04094 I

Library of Congress Catalog
Card Number 72-92428

Planning and Co-ordination: Sue Jacquemier
Research: Bridget Hadaway
Printed in Great Britain by:

Morrison & Gibb Ltd
London & Edinburgh

Cover picture: Allied soldier in the rubble of
Monte Cassino, Italy.
Back cover picture: German scout team on
patrol in the desert of North Africa.

Contents

Introduction

In World War Two, Germany and Japan fought in order to dominate large areas of the world. Great Britain, France, the United States and the other Allies entered the war reluctantly. For several years, Britain and France had made concessions to Germany in the hope of avoiding war and right up to September 3, 1939, both hoped that war could be avoided. The Soviet Union occupied part of Poland early in the war but entered the war on the side of the Allies in 1941.

The war itself was won and lost largely on the capacity to produce war material and the Allies, with the great arsenal of the United States behind them, were bound to win if they could withstand the early assaults. They were pushed to the brink of defeat but somehow they held on.

The war ended in an uneasy peace, with the West already distrustful of the Soviet Union and, in 1954, Britain's war leader, Winston Churchill, wrote of "how the great democracies triumphed and so were able to resume the follies which had so nearly cost them their life." Yet, in spite of all, World War Two ushered in more than a quarter of a century of peace between the major powers that still continues.

▽ **A German water-proofed tank.** These were used with great success in the first weeks of Operation *Barbarossa*, June 1941, when Hitler invaded Russia.

Note: In this book, all foreign words, names of ships, titles of poems and songs are in *italics*, e.g. HMS *Cornwallis*.

Declaration of War

It was quarter past eleven on Sunday morning, September 3, 1939. All over Britain, groups of people were gathered before radio sets. They heard the sombre voice of the Prime Minister, Neville Chamberlain, saying:

"This morning, the British Ambassador in Berlin handed the German Government a note stating that unless we heard from them by eleven o'clock that they were prepared to withdraw their troops from Poland, a state of war would exist between us. No such undertaking has been received and consequently this country is at war with Germany."

World War Two had begun. It is said that the seeds of the war were sown at the end of World War One with the Treaty of Versailles. The people of Germany felt that the peace terms were harsh. From 1933, their resentment was fanned into flames by a new and ruthless leader, Adolf Hitler.

In 1933, he withdrew Germany from the League of Nations. Two years later he openly announced that he intended to build up Germany's fighting forces. In 1936 he re-occupied the Rhineland, a border zone between Germany and France from which German forces were barred at the end of World War One.

By 1938, Germany had a strong army which marched into Austria and made that country part of the German *Reich* (empire). Next, Hitler claimed the Sudetenland, an area of Czechoslovakia bordering on Germany. Britain and France agreed to an alteration of the borders but, in March 1939, the Germans marched into the rest of the country and Hitler announced "Czechoslovakia has ceased to exist."

On September 1, 1939, Germany invaded Poland. Britain and France had promised to help the Poles. Once Britain had declared war, France acted. By 5 p.m. she was at war with Germany and before the day was over, so were Australia, New Zealand and India.

Canada, too, was preparing to enter the war on Britain's side but the United States decided to remain neutral.

△ **Adolf Hitler** (left) became Chancellor (Prime Minister) of Germany in 1933. 86-year-old **Field-Marshal Paul von Hindenburg** (right), a popular figure since World War One, was President. When Hindenburg died in 1934, Hitler became sole master of Germany. He had disposed of all his rivals by killing them or sending them into prison camps. He was known as the *Führer* (Leader).

△ **On October 1, 1938, Neville Chamberlain,** Prime Minister of Britain, flew home from a meeting in Munich, Germany, with Adolf Hitler. To cheering crowds, he waved a piece of paper. It was a document signed by Hitler promising that the peoples of Britain and Germany would never go to war with one another again. "I believe," said Chamberlain, "it is peace in our time," and he became a national hero. But within a year, World War Two had begun. In May, 1940 Chamberlain was forced to resign and he died before the year was out.

△ **This map shows the areas involved in Hitler's expansion that led to World War Two.** His aggression began on March 7, 1936, when German troops marched into the Rhineland. Hitler said later, "The 48 hours after the march into the Rhineland were the most nerve-racking of my life. If the French had marched, we would have had to withdraw with our tails between our legs." But the French did not march. The Germans built strong defences—the Siegfried Line—in the Rhineland, and turned their eyes on other areas—Austria, Czechoslovakia and the so-called "Polish Corridor" around Danzig.

△ **A cavalry unit of the Polish Army**—hopelessly out of date in terms of modern warfare. By contrast, Germany gave the world a new word in the invasion of Poland—*blitzkrieg,* meaning ''lightning-war.'' This was based on the use of swift-moving armoured vehicles.

△ **In Britain, special editions of the Sunday newspapers** were on sale on September 3, 1939; there was no TV and not everyone had a radio. Before the day was out, the first British lives had been lost. The liner *Athenia,* bound for Canada with 1,470 passengers, was torpedoed by a U-boat and 112 people were drowned.

▽ **German Mark IV tank**—a few were used in Germany's blitzkrieg along with Mark II and Mark III tanks. On September 1, 1939, German *Stuka* dive-bombers attacked Polish troops and military targets. Meanwhile tanks and infantry in vehicles thrust through the Polish lines. The aim was to overrun as much territory as possible in a short time. The Germans used six armoured divisions and eight other mobile divisions backed by 27 infantry divisions.

The War in the North

△ **Marshal Carl Mannerheim,** Commander-in-Chief of the Finns in the Winter War of 1939-40. He had learned his trade as an officer in the Russian Army, during the Russo-Japanese War of 1904-5 and World War One (1914-18). In 1939, his total forces numbered only 33,000.

△ **Finnish troops** travelled on skis and they used reindeer to help them. In their white clothing they were almost invisible against the snow and often took the Russians by surprise. The Russians were short of ski troops and white camouflage clothing. Their vehicles and equipment were not suited to the bitter winter cold. Hence, no *blitzkrieg*.

By tradition, Germany and the Soviet Union were enemies, each fearing the growth of the other's strength. But on August 23, 1939, they surprised the world by signing an agreement not to attack each other.

Then, on September 17, 1939, the Soviet Union invaded Poland from the east. This helped the Germans to complete the conquest of Poland by September 27. Afterwards, Germany and the Soviet Union divided the country between them.

Hitler did not at once attack elsewhere. What followed in the West was called the "phoney war". But on November 30 the Soviet Union made a move in the North. She launched an invasion of Finland. It was an unequal struggle. Finland's population was only 3½ million, the Soviet Union's 180 million. The Soviet Union had 9,000 tanks to Finland's 50. But the "Winter War", as it was called, was no *blitzkrieg*. It was more than three months before the Finns gave in.

On April 9, 1940, Germany struck again. Without warning, she began a seaborne invasion of Norway. Allied troops went to help the Norwegians but they could not prevent the conquest of Norway. It was all over by June. Denmark, also invaded on April 9, put up no resistance.

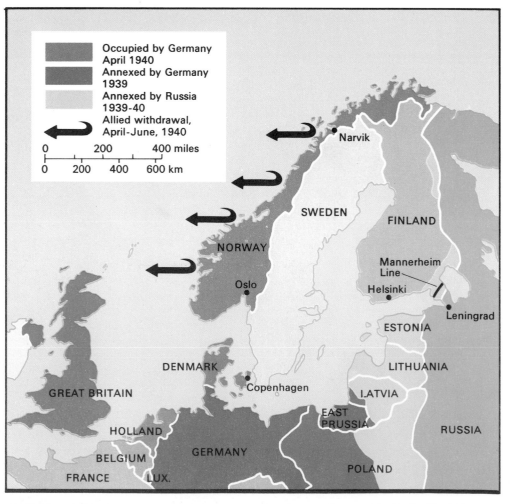

△ **At the end of the war in the north,** Germany had gained the long coastline of Norway for U-boat bases and airfields. From these, Allied shipping could be attacked in the North Sea and in the Atlantic.

△ **Speed of troop movements** was the essence of Germany's plan. In Norway they used paratroops like these. One airborne attack was launched on Oslo.

△ **Wrecked ships clog the harbour at Narvik.** In two sea battles, on April 10 and 13, British warships sank ten German destroyers for the loss of two. British, French and Polish troops recaptured Narvik from the Germans on May 28 in the first clear Allied land victory of the war. But events on the Western Front made the Allies decide to abandon Norway.

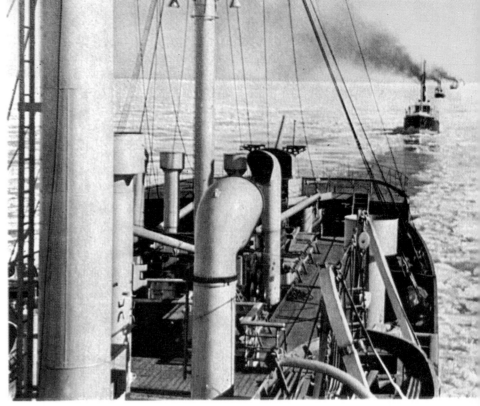

△**German transport ships** carrying troops and stores to Norway. On April 8 the Allies said they had laid mines in Norwegian waters to keep out German battleships and U-boats. At this time, some German troops were hidden in merchant ships in Norwegian ports and the invasion armada was already on its way.

▽ **German soldiers** in a burning village in Norway. The Norwegians fought bravely, hoping for help from the Allies. The Allies made three landings and for a time reclaimed Narvik. But they were forced to withdraw in June, 1940.

Hitler Strikes in the West

△ **In the attack against Holland,** the Germans used several battalions of paratroops.

On the Western Front, the "phoney war" went on into 1940. Neither France nor Britain was in a position to launch an attack against Germany. In the years between the wars, they had both run down their fighting forces.

They had seen the danger from Germany too late. They waited behind the Maginot Line for the German attack. But when the assault came, on May 10, 1940, it was on the two neutral countries of Holland and Belgium. Before dawn the *Luftwaffe* (German Air Force) made widespread bombing raids. Then, in Holland, paratroops landed and seized key bridges. An avalanche of tanks and infantry poured over the borders, and in four days it was all over. The Dutch surrendered.

Allied troops had advanced into Holland and Belgium but they were unable to halt the Germans. One thrust beginning 100 miles north of the Maginot Line drove into France and split the Allied armies into two. On May 18 the Belgians surrendered.

In the north of France, the British and the French First Army retreated to Dunkirk, bombed and machine-gunned by the *Luftwaffe* and pounded by artillery fire. Meantime, every available boat in the South of England—fishing boats, pleasure steamers, private yachts —put to sea along with 220 ships of the Royal Navy. On May 26–27 these boats rescued 338,000 troops from the beach at Dunkirk.

The French armies collapsed, and on June 21 the French asked for peace. But one high-ranking officer, General de Gaulle, escaped to Britain and formed the Free French Army.

A TYPICAL MAGINOT FORT

▽ **A British general, Alan Brooke, described France's Maginot Line as "a battleship built on land."** It was a massive concrete defence zone stretching from Switzerland in the south to the Forest of Ardennes in Belgium, and it took nearly ten years to build in the 1930's. The rooms in it were air-conditioned and underground railways carried troops and supplies from place to place. But it gave the French generals a "Maginot mentality"—a misguided faith in an impassable defence line. Their ideas belonged to World War One and they did not understand the notion of *blitzkrieg*.

Worse, France was wide open to an attack through Belgium because the defences did not extend along the Belgian frontier. A German armoured column struck into the hilly Ardennes country. It advanced swiftly. A line of French pillboxes on the River Meuse was battered by low-level bombing and the armour poured across the river towards the heart of France, *behind* the Maginot Line.

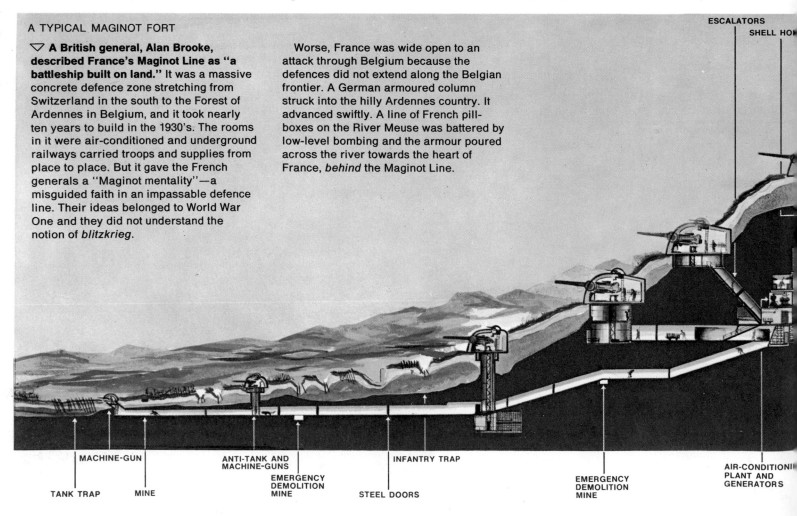

ESCALATORS
SHELL HO[...]

MACHINE-GUN

ANTI-TANK AND MACHINE-GUNS

INFANTRY TRAP

EMERGENCY DEMOLITION MINE

AIR-CONDITIONI[...] PLANT AND GENERATORS

TANK TRAP   MINE

EMERGENCY DEMOLITION MINE

STEEL DOORS

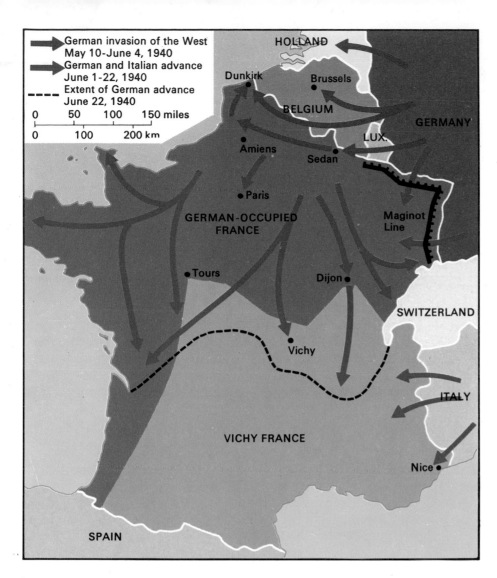

German invasion of the West
May 10-June 4, 1940

German and Italian advance
June 1-22, 1940

Extent of German advance
June 22, 1940

0   50   100   150 miles

0   100   200 km

HOLLAND

Dunkirk

Brussels

BELGIUM

GERMANY

Amiens

LUX.

Sedan

Paris

GERMAN-OCCUPIED
FRANCE

Maginot
Line

Tours

Dijon

SWITZERLAND

Vichy

ITALY

VICHY FRANCE

Nice

SPAIN

△ **People in Britain called this the "Miracle of Dunkirk"** and were proud of the "little ships" which saved so many lives. But Winston Churchill reminded them, "Wars are not won by evacuations".

◁ **Western Europe, June 22, 1940.** After the fall of France. Hitler said, "I can see no reason why this war must go on." He was ready to offer peace terms to Britain. Britain was not interested. Churchill had said, "We shall defend our island whatever the cost may be. We shall fight on the beaches, we shall fight in the fields and in the streets, we shall fight in the hills; we shall never surrender."

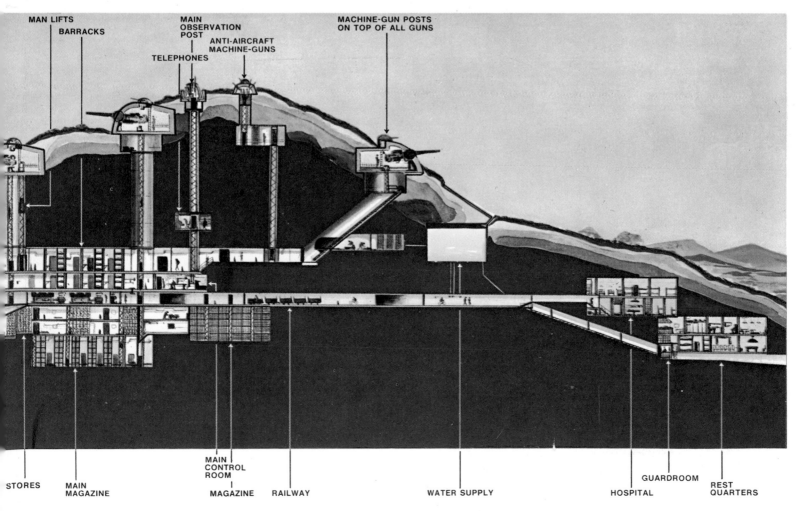

MAN LIFTS

BARRACKS

MAIN
OBSERVATION
POST

TELEPHONES

ANTI-AIRCRAFT
MACHINE-GUNS

MACHINE-GUN POSTS
ON TOP OF ALL GUNS

STORES

MAIN
MAGAZINE

MAIN
CONTROL
ROOM

MAGAZINE

RAILWAY

WATER SUPPLY

GUARDROOM

HOSPITAL

REST
QUARTERS

The Battle of Britain

△ **1940 picture of Winston Churchill** on a visit to the "front-line" at Dover. Seeing the vital need for more aircraft, Churchill made the dynamic Lord Beaverbrook Minister of Aircraft Production—and production accelerated. During the Battle of Britain and the "Blitz", as it was called, on London, Churchill's words and example held Britain together. Afterwards he said of the fighter pilots of the R.A.F., "Never in the field of human conflict was so much owed by so many to so few."

The words "Achtung! Spitfeuer!" ("Look out! Spitfire!") were often heard over the radio from German fighter pilots between July and October 1940.

The Supermarine Spitfire and the Hawker Hurricane were the chief British fighters used in the Battle of Britain, soon after the fall of France.

By this time, Hitler was willing to launch Operation *Sealion*—the invasion of Britain—and on July 2 the German High Command issued an order. It called for the control of the Channel seaway by the German navy and the destruction of the Royal Air Force.

The Battle opened with German bombers attacking British ships in the Channel. But they met with stiff opposition from R.A.F. fighters.

In August the Germans began bombing airfields in the South of England but each day their losses mounted. Over the Channel and the land on either side, aerial dog-fights developed between British Spitfires and Hurricanes and German Messerschmitt 109's. Between September 1 and 5, the Germans made eleven major attacks on fighter airfields and aircraft factories. Their losses were high. The R.A.F. claimed 562 destroyed for the loss of 219.

On September 7 the Germans launched a mass raid on London—320 bombers with an escort of 600 fighters followed by 250 more bombers. The attack started in daylight and went on all night. Next day there was another heavy attack.

Attacks on London went on daily and on September 15 came the heaviest daylight attack. But 56 German aircraft were shot down and this was the turning point. After October 5 no bombers ventured over Britain in daylight.

By October 12 it was clear that the R.A.F. had won the Battle of Britain. The *Luftwaffe* had lost 1,733 aircraft. Hitler cancelled Operation *Sealion*.

△ **British rescue worker** and victim of an air-raid. Goering called the raids on London "a stroke right into the enemy's heart." But it failed to shake the British will to win.

△ **Supermarine Spitfire.** Top speed: 361 m.p.h. Armament eight .303 in. machine-guns. It was replacing the Hurricane as the standard R.A.F. fighter.

△ **Messerschmitt 109E.** Top speed: 357 m.p.h. Armament: two 7.7 mm. machine guns, two 20 mm. cannon. Less manoeuvrable than the Spitfire and handicapped by short range.

△ **Hawker Hurricane.** Top speed: 328 m.p.h. Armament: eight .303 in. machine-guns. Britain's first monoplane fighter.

◁ **London street after air raid,** September 1940. This was the final phase of the Battle of Britain, when Goering, head of the *Luftwaffe,* pinned his hopes of success on terror raids. The first targets had been British shipping in the English Channel. Next came raids on airfields in the South and aircraft factories. Finally the "Blitz" on London.

Aircraft losses, 1940	Britain	Germany Claimed by RAF	Admitted by L'waffe
July	58	203	164
August	360	1,133	662
September	361	1,108	582
October	136	254	325
Total:	**915**	**2,698**	**1,733**

▽ **Dornier 215 German twin-engined bomber** used in strikes during Battle of Britain. Top speed: 311 m.p.h. Bomb load: 2,215 lb. Engines: two Daimler-Benz. Though fast enough to lead the British fighters a chase, the Do-215 had a weak defence armament and carried a poor bomb-load. Developed from the pre-war Do-17, and nicknamed the "Flying Pencil."

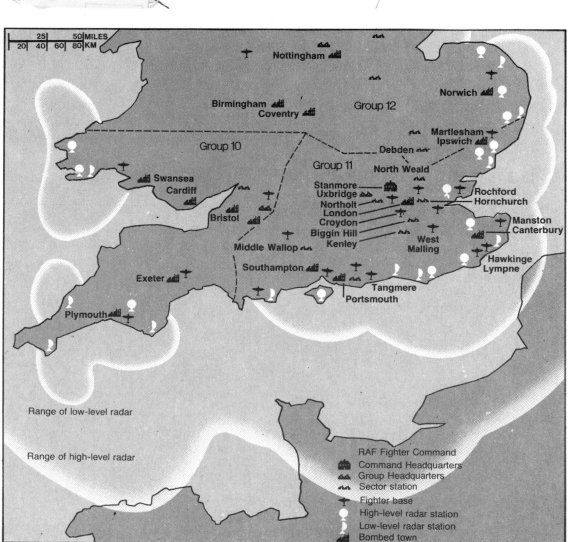

△ **Two key parts of a radar set:** a magnetron, a valve the size of a child's fist, invented by Sir John Randall; and a copper anode (terminal).

	RAF Fighter Command
🏛	Command Headquarters
🏛	Group Headquarters
⚓	Sector station
✈	Fighter base
○	High-level radar station
○	Low-level radar station
🏭	Bombed town

◁ **The geography of the Battle of Britain.** The radar stations were a well-kept secret in 1940. From 1935, a team of scientists was racing to perfect a system of radar and install the stations on the coast. By the start of the war, aircraft could be detected 150 miles away. As a result, in the Battle of Britain, fighter planes and their pilots could be kept on the ground until they were needed instead of having to patrol. The R.A.F. had only half as many planes as the *Luftwaffe.* Radar helped to level the odds.

Bombing

At the start of World War Two, high-ranking air force personnel on both sides believed that they could smash the enemy's war machine by a bomber blitz.

The Germans had to revise their ideas of what could be achieved by bombers after the Battle of Britain, and, when the tide turned for the Allies, they still had to learn how best to use air strikes into the heart of Occupied Europe.

In the early stages of the war they used "area bombing" of industrial cities. It had two aims: (a) to reduce war production, and (b) to lower morale. It did neither. War production still rose and people became more determined not to lose the war

One example of a concentrated bombing attack on a city was that made on Coventry on November 14–15, 1940. Churchill wept at the devastation but it only stiffened Britain's resolve to fight on.

In the last year of the war, bombers of the R.A.F. and United States Army Air Force began to carry out precision bombing raids on key targets. The U.S.A.A.F. laid on 1,000-aircraft daylight raids. These finally had an effect. Germany's oil production was almost destroyed and her transport system severely damaged.

One of the final major air attacks of the war in the West was a succession of bombing raids on Dresden on February 13–14, 1945. Over 800 aircraft took part and added one more to the number of German cities almost totally destroyed.

△ **The Möhne Dam** breached by the British "Dam Busters" in one of the most famous raids of the war on May 16-17, 1943. 19 Lancasters, led by Wing-Commander Guy Gibson, attacked five dams in the industrial Ruhr using special bombs. The Möhne Dam and the Eder were both breached, the Sorpe Dam damaged. Almost a quarter of the air crew on the raid were killed. The raid is now known to have achieved little.

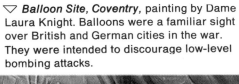

▽ **Balloon Site, Coventry,** painting by Dame Laura Knight. Balloons were a familiar sight over British and German cities in the war. They were intended to discourage low-level bombing attacks.

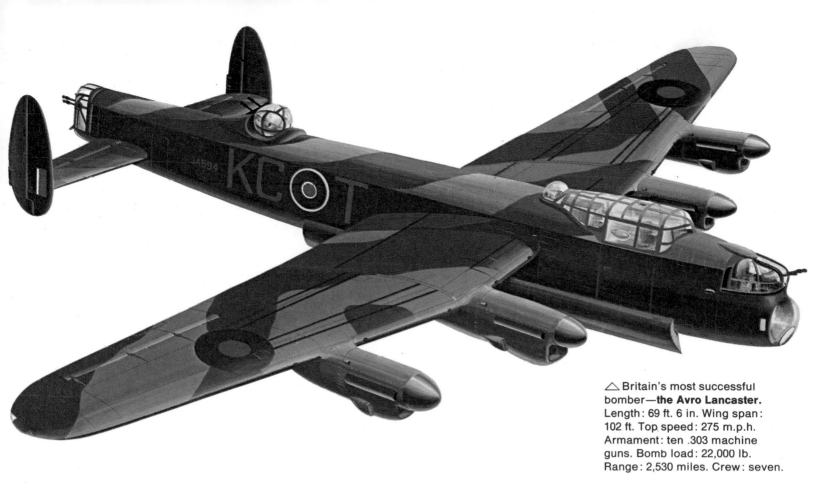

△ Britain's most successful bomber—**the Avro Lancaster.** Length: 69 ft. 6 in. Wing span: 102 ft. Top speed: 275 m.p.h. Armament: ten .303 machine guns. Bomb load: 22,000 lb. Range: 2,530 miles. Crew: seven.

◁ **Bomb damage in Hanover.** In one raid, in October 1943, $2\frac{1}{2}$ square miles of the city were destroyed. In all, 15,000 tons of bombs were dropped on Hanover, compared with the top figure of 50,000 tons on Berlin. Most of Germany's big cities were laid waste. In Cologne, 60 per cent of the homes were destroyed. Yet the Germans, like the British, were not dispirited by bombing. Almost to the end, it made them more determined not to give in.

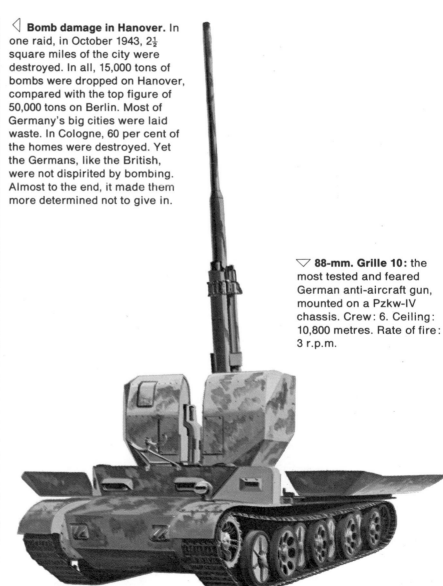

▽ **88-mm. Grille 10:** the most tested and feared German anti-aircraft gun, mounted on a Pzkw-IV chassis. Crew: 6. Ceiling: 10,800 metres. Rate of fire: 3 r.p.m.

Attack on the Balkans

Eastern Europe 1941—severe blows for the Allies. But British Foreign Minister Anthony Eden believed the war was won and lost here—Allied heroism delayed the German invasion of Russia.

Map legend:
- Italy and annexed territory, 1939
- Occupied by Axis Powers, 1941
- Annexed by Germany
- Axis satellite countries, 1941

▽ **German heavy anti-aircraft gun emplacement** on the Bulgaria-Greece frontier. On March 1, 1941, Bulgaria agreed to join the Tripartite Pact, thus entering World War Two on the side of the Axis. The pact was among Germany, Italy and Japan and had been signed on 28 September, 1940. Before Bulgaria joined the pact, the German Twelfth Army under Field-Marshal List was in Bulgaria getting ready to attack Greece.

Benito Mussolini, dictator of Italy, declared war on the Allies on June 10, 1940, when France was on the brink of defeat, and sent troops into Southern France.

Italy played a bigger part when, later in the year, the Axis powers turned their attention to the Balkans (and later still, to Africa: *cf* p. 16). German troops occupied Rumania without a fight but, when Mussolini threatened Greece, she gave him a defiant reply. So he sent 200,000 troops to attack Greece from Albania (which Italy had taken over in 1939).

With help rushed out from Britain, the Greeks counter-attacked and, by the end of December, they had captured a quarter of Albania. Hitler, concerned at his ally's failure, decide to intervene.

On March 1, 1941, Bulgaria allowed German troops to pass through the country but Yugoslavia refused to join the Axis and, on April 6, Germany invaded Yugoslavia. After ten days of *blitzkrieg*, the Yugoslavs gave in.

Meanwhile, the Germans had also invaded Greece. In spite of help from a small British army, the Greeks surrendered on April 21, and the British army escaped by sea.

Germany's next target was the large Greek island of Crete. After bombing the airfields, the Germans invaded the island by air on May 20 using paratroops and troop-carrying gliders. Eight days later it was clear that the Allies could not hold Crete. The Royal Navy began taking troops off. The *Luftwaffe* established air bases on Crete. From these they could control the air over the eastern Mediterranean.

German air power posed a tremendous threat to Allied shipping. However, there was no trouble from the Italian Fleet. Caught at sea on March 28, 1941, it took a battering in the Battle of Cape Matapan (Greece) and did not venture forth again.

△ **German troops capture and disarm Yugoslav guerilla fighters.** The Germans invaded with 33 divisions, six armoured. The Yugoslavs had 28 including three out-of-date cavalry divisions.

▷ **German Dornier bomber** over the Acropolis in Athens. As the British army retreated, thousands of people lined the streets cheering, throwing flowers and shouting "You will be back. We'll be waiting for you." The Germans took Athens on April 27, 1941. The British returned in October 1944.

▽ **Defeated Greek prisoners** under German guard. A wounded soldier is carried by his comrades.

△ **Anti-aircraft gun crew on Malta,** a small island lying 60 miles south of Sicily. It was a key naval base. On the day Italy declared war, it suffered the first of the 1,000 air raids made on the island during the next two and a half years. For a time its sole defenders were three Gloster Gladiators nicknamed "Faith", "Hope" and "Charity".

Italy Loses an Empire

At the start of World War Two, Italy had a developing empire. To parts of Africa she had owned since World War One–Libya, Eritrea and Italian Somaliland–she had added Ethiopia (conquered in 1936), and, in Europe, Albania (taken over in 1939).

On August 5, 1940 Italy launched successful attacks on British and French Somaliland. As the Allied troops left, Mussolini proclaimed "a magnificent victory" for Italian arms.

But the struggle in Africa was only just beginning. At Allied GHQ in Cairo, General Wavell planned the defence of Egypt and re-conquest in East Africa. An Italian army was poised on the Libyan border, but, as they did not attack, the Allies began a raid on the Italian lines in December 1940.

The Italians were routed, and the Allies drove them back across the Western Desert to beyond Benghazi. In 62 days, the Allies took 130,000 prisoners and captured 380 tanks and 845 field guns. It was the Allies' first major victory on land in World War Two.

Meanwhile, in January 1941, Allied troops invaded Eritrea, and broke the Italian resistance by April. The invasion of Ethiopia began in January; the Allies were soon advancing at a surprising rate—1,054 miles in 35 days—and the main Italian forces surrendered on May 18. Italian Somaliland was also overrun and Mussolini had lost almost all of his empire.

△ **German airmen** resting beside their aircraft in the desert. When Rommel and the Afrika Korps arrived in the Libyan Desert, *Luftwaffe* fighters and bombers gave them all-round air superiority over the Allies for a time and played an important part in the successes that built up the legend of Rommel as a great commander.

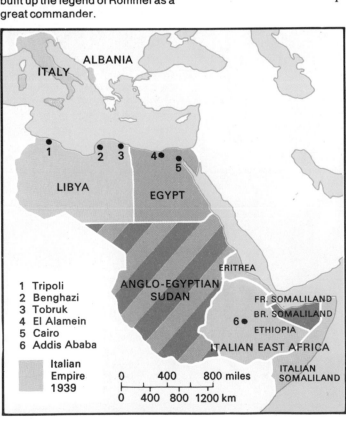

1 Tripoli
2 Benghazi
3 Tobruk
4 El Alamein
5 Cairo
6 Addis Ababa

▷ **The war in Africa.** The fighting in Libya became a seesaw struggle in 1941-42. Tripoli, Benghazi and Tobruk were major prizes in any advance. Addis Ababa, capital of Ethiopia, was re-entered by the emperor, Haile Selassie, on May 5th, 1941. Said Churchill, "The first lawful sovereign to be driven from his throne by the Fascist-Nazi criminals, the first to return in triumph."

▷ **British soldiers taken prisoner** in Libya by the Germans. The struggle in the Libyan Desert was to go on for two years after Wavell's victorious campaign. In February 1941, the German Afrika Korps arrived commanded by General Rommel, soon to be known as the "Desert Fox". In the spring of 1941, Rommel pushed back the Allies.

△ **January 1941.** Fire rages in Tobruk as Australian soldiers inspect tanks captured from the retreating Italians.

△ **Members of the Afrika Korps** in a German staff car.

▽ **Infantry Mk II.** Armour: 78-mm. Turret gun: 2-pounder. In the rout of the Italians in Libya in 1940-41, tanks like this one, nick-named the "Matilda", played a big part.

The Home Front

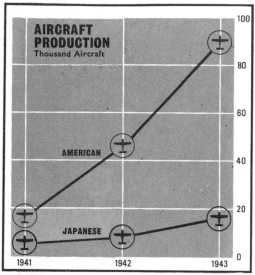

△ **This graph shows how aircraft production** in the United States outstripped that in Japan and made victory in the Pacific War inevitable for the Allies.

△ **Flying Fortresses** being mass-produced in U.S.A. The United States produced more war material than all of the Axis countries put together.

△ **Woman doing war work** on a shell production line in Japan.

In World War Two, as in no previous war, civilians outside the battle areas were involved in the conflict through air raids.

Towns were blacked out. No street lights were lit and it was forbidden to allow light to escape from windows.

From the autumn of 1940 people in Britain were wakened by the wail of the warning sirens, heard the sound of aircraft engines overhead and of falling bombs. They watched the night sky lit with the flames of burning buildings and next day saw gaping ruins in their streets. 100,000 civilians, including air raid wardens, firemen and other members of the auxiliary services, died in the United Kingdom.

Germany's ordeal by air raids came later. In France and other occupied countries, civilians knew the horrors of war at first hand and also the grimness of life under a conqueror.

In Europe, civilians had to suffer the rationing of food and clothing. In the United States they were luckier. Production kept pace with the needs of the home front as well as those of the armed forces.

In most countries women worked in war factories to boost the output of much-needed war materials. 75,000 girls joined the Women's Land Army in Britain and helped to grow more food. In Britain, food rationing started in January 1940 but it had already begun in Germany in September 1939.

Railings disappeared from the streets of Britain—melted down to make munitions. In Germany, bells were melted down, in France statues.

Civilians in Germany were forbidden to listen to broadcasts by the Allies, but in Britain, people listened openly to "Lord Haw Haw" from Berlin and treated him as a huge joke.

△ **British girls help after explosion of V-bomb** towards war's end. Women played a major part in Britain's war effort. As ambulance drivers, many were heroines of the "Blitz". Others served in the Women's Royal Naval Service, the Auxiliary Territorial Service or the Women's Auxiliary Air Force.

△ **German food ration** for one person for one week. Bread: 2,425 grammes, cereals 150, potatoes 3,500, sugar 225, jam or honey 175, meat 250, fats 185, cheese 60, coffee 60, half an egg, skim milk. In Britain, bread, cereals and potatoes were unrationed, and liquid milk was available.

◁ **French refugees** waiting to be transported to a new home. In Europe, the war uprooted countless families and left them homeless. At war's end, there were vast numbers of refugees and they created a problem for the Allies. Refugee camps were set up, and many of the people in them had heart-rending stories to tell.

△ **Woman working as a skilled machinist** in a munitions factory (a painting by Dame Laura Knight). Before the war, it would have been undreamt of for a woman to tackle such a job in Britain, but two million women undertook war work of all kinds. In Russia, women took on the toughest industrial work in the absence of men.

Hitler Invades Russia

In late 1940, with the Battle of Britain lost, yet with no threat from the Allies in the West, Hitler turned his mind in another direction. On December 18 he sent out nine copies of a secret document. It bore the code name Barbarossa.

The document began: "The German armed forces must be prepared to crush Soviet Russia in a quick campaign before the end of the war against England". Six months later thousands of tanks moved eastwards and, on June 22, 1941, Germany invaded Russia, expecting a speedy conquest.

At first things went well. Goering claimed that 3,000 Soviet planes were destroyed in the first week and by July 7 the Germans had taken 150,000 prisoners and captured 1,200 tanks. By July 10 the Germans had covered 400 miles in 18 days and were attacking Smolensk. Moscow, the capital, was only 200 miles ahead. But from Smolensk onwards Russian resistance hardened. More up-to-date planes challenged the *Luftwaffe*. The new Soviet T-34 tank was superior to any German tank.

In August the Germans struck southwards towards Kiev, aiming for the Crimea. The Germans captured Kiev on September 18. But winter was approaching and things were not going

as well as Hitler hoped.

On October 2 the drive for Moscow began and in three weeks the Germans were within 30 miles of the city. But the Russian winter broke early. Mud, snow and ice bogged down the armoured columns. The Germans were short of anti-freeze for their vehicles. The telescopic sights of tanks froze in sub-zero temperatures.

Yet the Germans had reached the suburbs of Moscow on December 2 before Marshal Zhukov launched a counter-attack and drove them back. For once, *blitzkrieg* had failed.

△ **Soviet partisans**—patriots who hid in the forests and marshes to attack the German invaders. In the winter of 1941-2 many of them died of hunger and cold, but by 1943 the guerilla fighters were better organized.

◁ When Germany invaded Russia, Churchill promised Josef Stalin, the Soviet dictator, support from Britain. Supplies were sent to Russia in convoys across the Arctic. Soon aircraft like this **Hawker Hurricane IIc** were facing the *Luftwaffe* on the Eastern Front. Top speed: 329 m.p.h. Armament: four 20-mm. cannon.

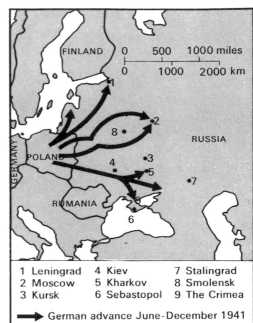

1 Leningrad	4 Kiev	7 Stalingrad
2 Moscow	5 Kharkov	8 Smolensk
3 Kursk	6 Sebastopol	9 The Crimea

➤ German advance June-December 1941

△ **The geography of** *Barbarossa*. The Germans retreated from Moscow on December 14, 1941. Zhukov's drive petered out in mid-February 1942, and a new German offensive began in June. On September 6 the German advance was halted at Stalingrad and the scene was set for one of the key battles of the war. The Germans had already paid a heavy price—1,167,835 casualties by April 30, 1942. Worse was to come . . .

△ **German soldiers in winter dress** in a snow-clad landscape. Not all the German troops were well-equipped to withstand the sub-zero temperatures. They were fighting in unfamiliar climatic conditions, whereas the Russians were used to the bitterness of winter.

▷ **Russian peasants fleeing before the German advance** on Moscow. By December 1941, 70 million people were living under German rule in Russia. The Germans treated civilians ruthlessly. Millions were sent to Germany as slaves or put to death. But they remained defiant.

▽ Artillery played a big part in the war for the Russians. Like this **76.2 mm. Type 39 Howitzer.** Range: 14,766 yds. Weight of shot: 13.75 lb.

Resistance and Sabotage

In all parts of Occupied Europe, there were groups of people who continued to oppose the Germans. They formed the Resistance – dedicated patriots prepared to risk torture and death in order to harass the occupying forces and assist the Allies.

As the war went on the groups became more highly organized. They received weapons and supplies and they helped Allied agents to carry out their missions. In time, they became parts of organizations built up in Britain by the Special Operations Executive (S.O.E.)

In France and Belgium, the Resistance organized escape routes of Allied airmen shot down over occupied territory. Everywhere the Resistance took part in activities to undermine the German war effort—sabotage in factories, the destruction of railway engines and bridges, the disruption of transport.

In France by early 1944, 100,000 Resistance fighters were ready to take a more active part in the struggle for freedom and groups called the *Maquis* were already fighting against the Germans. Intelligence nets were transmitting information of use to the Allies.

In Norway in 1943, Resistance fighters put a heavy-water plant out of action and held up the German atomic research programme.

△ **Violette Bushell** was born in Paris on June 26, 1921. Her father was English, her mother French. At the start of the war she was a shop assistant in London. She married an officer in the French Foreign Legion, Etienne Szabo, and he was killed in the Battle of Alamein. Leaving her daughter, Violette trained as a secret agent. In April 1944 she was flown into France on her first secret mission.

The Resistance called her "Corinne". On the night of June 6, 1944, she parachuted into France to work with the *Maquis*. Captured, she was sent to Ravensbruck concentration camp and there executed. She was awarded the *Croix de Guerre* and the George Cross.

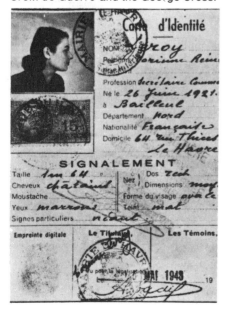

▷ **Secret printing press at work in Paris.** The production of pamphlets like those above was important for the morale of the Resistance. In Belgium over 300 secret newspapers were printed during the occupation. On November 9, 1943, 100,000 copies of a fake edition of the German controlled *Le Soir* were printed and sold on newsstands all over the country. The Germans were furious.

△ **Josip Broz, who called himself Marshal Tito,** leader of guerilla fighters in Occupied Yugoslavia. After the fall of Yugoslavia in April 1941, Tito and his *Partisans* fought on, keeping 30 Axis divisions busy and having a price of 100,000 gold marks set on his head. General Mihailovich also led a group of guerillas called *Chetniks*. By 1943 Tito had survived five Axis offensives against him. Then Allied observers landed in Yugoslavia and decided help should be sent to him.

△ **Group of Tito's *Partisans*** on a march across the mountains of Yugoslavia. They fought the *Chetniks* as well as the Axis forces, saying the *Chetniks* were helping the Germans. From 1943 British officers were dropped by parachute to help Tito. Supplies and weapons were airlifted in. When the Russians swept into the Balkans in late 1944, Tito's forces linked up with them to liberate Belgrade.

△ **Some S.O.E. tools for espionage and sabotage.**
1 Radio transceiver (British). **2** Headphones for transceiver. **3** Silent pistol. **4** Radio transmitter. **5** Power pack. **6** Receiver. **7** Aerial. **8** Adaptor for transmitter, power pack, receiver. **9** Indian wrist dagger. **10** Kodak camera (adapted for documents). **11** Rega Minox camera. **12** German igniter (operated by pressure). **13** Delayed action pencil detonators. **14** German igniter (operated by pull). **15** Gas-pistol pencil. **16** British igniter (operated by lifter weight). **17** Medicine tube (for concealing detonators). **18** Hand-pump torch.

Only 3,000 pounds of explosives were used for the 150 most successful acts of sabotage in factories in France in 1943-44. This is equal to the load of one Mosquito bomber—which shows how effective sabotage is. One Resistance group in Belgium put all high tension electricity lines out of action at the same time.

The Battle of the Atlantic

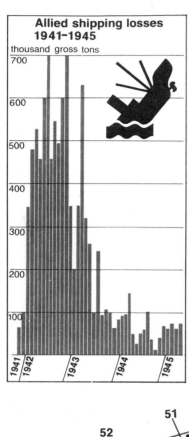

Allied shipping losses 1941-1945
thousand gross tons

The Battle of the Atlantic was an important factor right through the war. "Never for one moment could we forget that everything elsewhere depended on its outcome," said Churchill.

Britain needed to import food, raw materials for the factories, and fuel to keep aircraft, ships and land vehicles in action. In addition, from March 1941, increasing amounts of war material were sent across the Atlantic from the United States.

From the start, the Germans pinned their hopes of victory on U-boats. In August 1939 the submarine-packs put to sea and, on war's first day, the liner *Athenia* was sunk. In an attempt to thwart the U-boats, Allied merchant ships sailed in convoys with armed escorts.

But at first the escorts were inadequate. A convoy of 60 ships might be escorted by a single destroyer. The losses were appalling. In 1942, 1,160 Allied ships were lost.

But gradually, with more warships, more aircraft and better anti-submarine devices, the situation improved. In August 1943, more U-boats were destroyed (74) than ships sunk (58). The Battle was by no means over, but at last the Allies were winning.

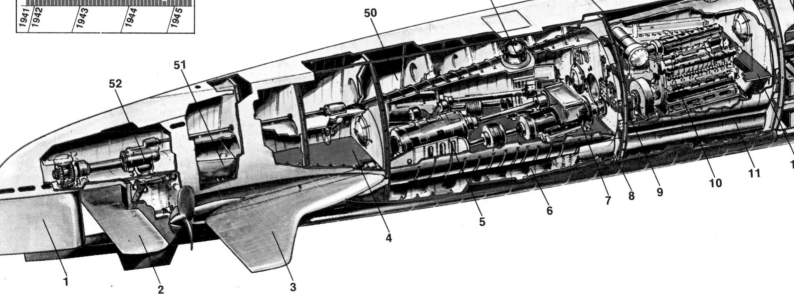

△ **Depth charges: 1** Dropped over stern. **2** Ready to be fired. **3** Carrier falls away. **4** Shock waves strike U-boat. **5** Pattern of charges seeking U-boat.

1 Rudder. 2 Aft Hydroplane. 3 Stern plane. 4 Aft emergency steering room. 5 Electric propulsion engines developing 226 Shaft Horse Power. 6 Fuel saddle tanks. 7 Gears for Electric engines. 8 Oil sump. 9 Diesel motor gears. 10 Main engine room containing two diesel engines developing 4,000 BHP and 5,000 SHP. 11 Ballast tank. 12 Catwalk giving repair access to the upper parts of the engine. 13 Accumulators. 14 Refrigerator. 15 Galley. 16 Starboard potato store; Port Ammunition store. 17 Periscope machinery. 18 Main control room. 19 Steering position. 20 Watertight bulkhead door. 21 Radio room. 22 Forward lower accumulator stores. 23 Junior officers' cabin. 24 Ballast blowing vents. 25 Torpedo crew quarters. 26 Upper forward accumulator room. 27 Compressed air bottle. 28 Torpedo storage room. 29 Six forward-firing torpedo tubes angled downwards to avoid enemy observation of

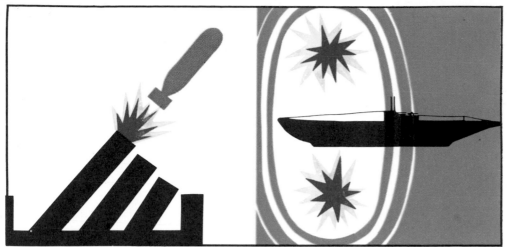

△ **Anti-submarine device: Squid.** It fired three bombs designed to explode under water around a U-boat. The concussion from them, if on target, would be sufficient to crack the U-boat's hull. Even a near-miss might be sufficient to force the U-boat to the surface.

torpedoes in the water. 30 Torpedo tube doors mechanism. 31 Forward pressure bulkhead. 32 Forward hydroplane. 33 Water- and pressure-tight torpedo loading hatch. 34 Space between twin hulls used as ballast container. 35 Forward main pressure hull. 36 Two 37-mm. guns. 37 Hatch into conning tower. 38 Periscope trunking. 39 Hatch to bridge. 40 Periscope pedestal. 41 Search periscope (raised). 42 Schnorkel. 43 Aerial. 44 Two 37-mm. guns. 45 Escape hatch. 46 Crew room. 47 Air trunking from schnorkel to engine room. 48 Engine room escape hatch. 50 Fuel tank. 51 After trim tank. 52 Rudder steering gear.

△ **German U-boat XXI.** Designed specifically to avoid detection by sub-hunters, it might have won back the advantage for Germany in the Battle of the Atlantic. Planned for delivery in 1944, the XXIs were not ready in time and the first only sailed on operations in April 1945. Length: 251 ft. 9 in. Beam: 21 ft. 9 in. Depth: 20 ft.

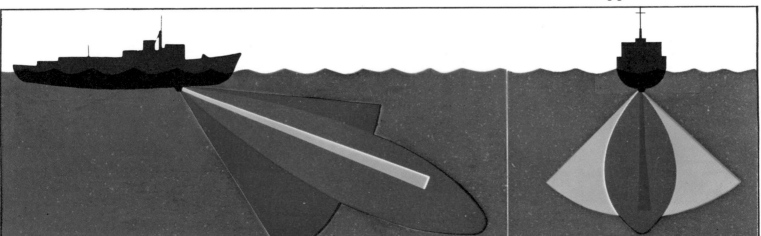

△ **Asdic, device used to locate U-boats.** It consisted of a transmitter/receiver which sent out sound impulses and picked up an echo if an impulse struck an object. By noting the time between the transmission and the echo, the range of the object could be worked out. Asdic used three impulses: 1 (orange) diffused over wide area, to locate U-boat; 2 (pink) narrow, vertical, and 3 (green) horizontal, to fix its position.

Pearl Harbour

At 7 a.m. on Sunday, December 7, 1941, a radar operator of the United States Army reported a large flight of aircraft about 130 miles from the naval base of Pearl Harbour on Oahu Island in the Pacific Ocean.

A junior officer read the report and took no action. The United States was not at war and he thought the aircraft must be friendly. But 55 minutes later an avalanche of bombs began to rain down on Pearl Harbour from high- and low-level bombers, while torpedo aircraft attacked ships in the harbour.

The aircraft were Japanese—386 of them from carriers at sea. By this act they showed that Japan was at war with the United States. The U.S. forces were not ready for the attack. It went on for over one hour almost without resistance.

The attack on Pearl Harbour brought the United States into World War Two. Twenty-four hours earlier President Roosevelt had been having peace talks with a Japanese envoy in Washington. Japan had signed a treaty with Germany and Italy in 1936 and in 1937 attacked China. As China and the United States were friends, this made Japan and the U.S. possible enemies.

After the fall of France, Japan seized French bases in Indo-China and began to build up her troops there. Britain feared an attack on Malaya and Singapore. The U.S. was ready to support the Allies with everything short of war. She cut off supplies of oil to Japan and asked Japan to withdraw her troops from China and Indo-China. This was what the peace talks were about, and the talking ended on December 7.

▽ **Map (below) of Japanese expansion, December 1941-May 1942.** Within hours of the attack on Pearl Harbour, Japanese bombers raided U.S. bases on the islands of Guam, Midway and Wake in the Pacific. They also bombed Manila in the Philippine Islands and the British base of Singapore.

In December Japanese troops landed on Luzon in the Philippines. About the same time Hong Kong, Guam and Wake Island were captured. To the surprise of the British, Japanese troops (some of them on bicycles) pushed through the thick jungle of the Malay Peninsula and attacked Singapore from the rear—all its defences pointed out to sea. On February 16, 1942, Singapore surrendered.

Eleven days later, the Japanese defeated the Allies in a naval battle in the Java Sea and swept on to take Sumatra, Java and the Dutch East Indies. In the Philippines, the U.S. forces, led by General Douglas MacArthur, put up a stubborn resistance. In March, President Roosevelt ordered MacArthur to Australia to take command of the defence of the South-West Pacific. As he left he made a vow he was to keep: "I shall return."

The troops left on the Bataan Peninsula ran out of food and surrendered on April 9. Others on the rocky island of Corregidor in Manila Bay held out until May 6. Afterwards the Japanese made 40,000 prisoners march 70 miles to prison camps, and over half of them died.

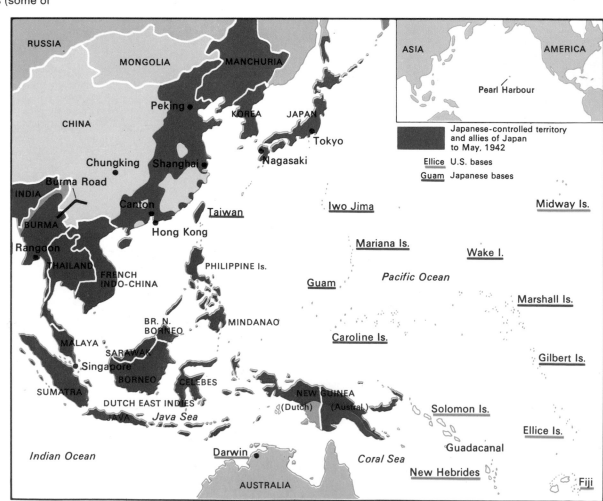

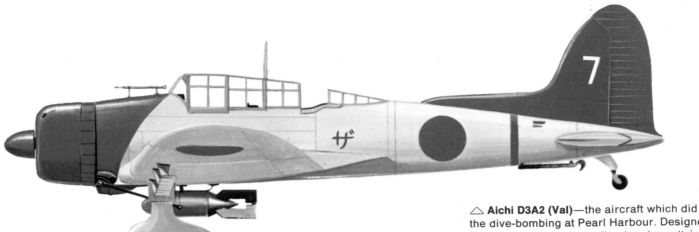

△ **Aichi D3A2 (Val)**—the aircraft which did the dive-bombing at Pearl Harbour. Designed like Germany's pre-war dive-bombers, it was Japan's first low-wing, all-metal monoplane dive-bomber.

Maximum range: 970 miles. Bomb load: 816 lb. Also used at Pearl Harbour were: Mitsubishi A6M2 Zero-sen (Zeke), the fastest fighter plane in the Pacific in 1941. Top speed: 351 m.p.h. Max. range: 975 miles. Armament: two 20-mm. cannon, two 7.7-mm. machine-guns, and the Nakajima B5N2 (Kate), a torpedo-bomber. Max. speed: 235 m.p.h. Max. range: 1,400 miles.

▽ **The destruction at Pearl Harbour.** There were eight battleships in the harbour. Three were sunk outright, one capsized, one was set on fire and the other three were badly damaged. Other ships were damaged, a mine-layer was sunk, three cruisers damaged, two destroyers sunk, another damaged. The air strike was made in two waves. In the first, Zeros machine-gunned the three airfields on Oahu while torpedo aircraft attacked the ballleships. In the second, heavy bombs were dropped from high-level bombers and dive-bombers. The second wave ran into some anti-aircraft fire but Japanese losses were only 29 aircraft. 173 U.S. aircraft were destroyed.

Guns and Tanks

In the closing stages of World War One, primitive tanks had shown the potentialities of a weapon first used in 1916 by the British.

In the inter-war years the techniques of tank warfare were studied, particularly by the Germans.

The tanks of World War Two were larger, more heavily armoured and more efficient, and as the war went on new types were introduced.

Artillery still had a part to play. The historic victory at El Alamein was pre-ceded by a tremendous artillery barrage. At Stalingrad in 1943, the Russians massed 4,000 field guns on a three-mile front—almost one gun a yard!

Small arms for infantry remained important, too, and included a multiplicity of automatic weapons, especially ones which could be mass-produced.

△ **German small arms. 1** KAW-98K 7.9-mm. rifle (five rounds in magazine). **2** MP-40 machine-pistol (32 rounds in magazine). **3** Walther P-38 9-mm. automatic (8 rounds in magazine). **4** Standard hand-grenade. A typical situation in which these weapons became vital to the infantryman was that which occurred at Stalingrad where house-to-house fighting took place.

▷ **The massive Sherman tank** first produced for the Allies in 1941 and afterwards to become their main tank. Mass production of this tank in the United States was vital to the success of the Allies in North Africa and Europe. Although some German tanks had superior guns and armour, none was more reliable than the Sherman.
Max. speed: 23 m.p.h. Range: 80 miles. Crew: 5. Weight: 71,900 lb. Engine: Chrysler model A57 (30-cylinder, 460-BHP). Armament: one 75-mm. M3 gun, one .30-inch machine-gun in hull, one .50-inch machine-gun on flexible mounting.

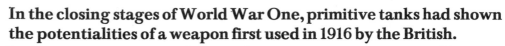

Commander's hatch
Gunner's shield
.30-inch machine-gun (hidden by breech)
Radio aerial socket
Radiator
Left fuel filler-cap
Chrysler 5-bank 30-cylinder 445-hp engine (1,253 cu. in.)
Cooling fan

▽ **German troops equipped for street fighting** in the rubble of the devastated city of Stalingrad. The tommy-gun and the hand-grenade proved to be key weapons. The defending Russians used teams equipped with a variety of weapons—light and heavy machine-guns, tommy-guns and grenades as well as anti-tank guns.

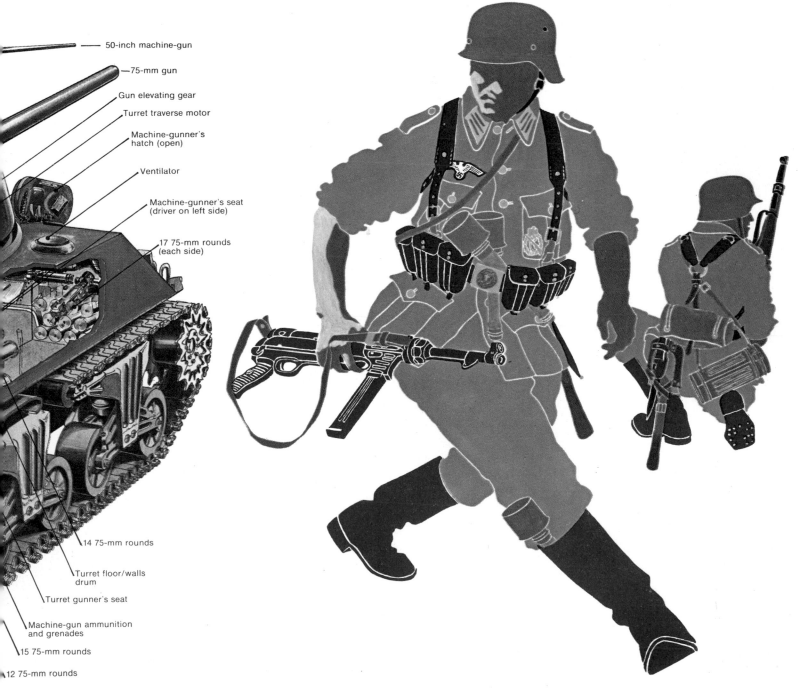

- 50-inch machine-gun
- 75-mm gun
- Gun elevating gear
- Turret traverse motor
- Machine-gunner's hatch (open)
- Ventilator
- Machine-gunner's seat (driver on left side)
- 17 75-mm rounds (each side)

- 14 75-mm rounds
- Turret floor/walls drum
- Turret gunner's seat
- Machine-gun ammunition and grenades
- 15 75-mm rounds
- 12 75-mm rounds

Japan Conquers the East

In 1942 Burma was part of the British Empire, but Britain was too hard-pressed in Europe to protect her distant possessions.

Indeed, during their 100 years in Burma, the British had paid little attention to the defence of the country. One month before the fall of Singapore, on January 15, Japanese invasion forces poured over the Burmese border from the south. Meanwhile Thailand made a treaty with the Japanese and more invaders advanced from Thailand.

In all Burma, there were only five R.A.F. squadrons, equipped with an obsolete fighter, the *Buffalo*, in addition to one American squadron from China. With practically no air cover, short of artillery and transport, ill-trained for jungle warfare, the Allied troops in Burma began the longest retreat in British history—900 miles to India.

At first the Japanese advanced rapidly and captured Rangoon, on March 9. By this time, the Chinese, under General Stilwell of the United States, were helping the British troops, which included Indians, Ghurkas and Burmese. Still forced to retreat, they fought for time. The monsoon would put an end to the fighting for a spell and the object now was to stop the Japanese from reaching India before the monsoon broke. Somehow, they succeeded.

On April 29 the Japanese drove across the Burma Road, cutting off supplies by land to China, and soon they crossed the River Chindwin, the last natural barrier before India. But on May 12 the monsoon broke.

Lt.-Gen. Slim, commander of the British forces, wrote later: "The monsoon whose rain beat mercilessly on our bodies did us one good turn—it stopped dead the Japanese pursuit." The long retreat ended, but Burma was lost.

△ **The Japanese soldier** was said to be able to fight and march on a handful of rice a day. Certainly he was efficient and well-equipped.

◁ **British troops taken prisoner by the Japanese.** Ahead of them: privation and misery. The Japanese paid little respect to the Geneva Convention's demands for the treatment of P.O.W.'s.

△ **Chiang Kai-shek** defied the Japanese from 1937.

△ **Japanese soldiers in an offensive in China.** They entered China on the pretext of an "unprovoked Chinese attack", and concealed the invasion from the West.

△ **Mao Tse-tung,** Communist guerilla leader against the Japanese.

The War in China

Japan invaded China on July 7, 1937, and the war in China was still going on when the Japanese attacked Pearl Harbour and entered World War Two. Under Generalissimo Chiang Kai-Shek, the Chinese put up a stubborn resistance and in 1942 they were keeping one million Japanese troops occupied—and out of the Pacific War.

From 1940, the United States helped the Chinese with material and military advice but Japan almost sealed off China by capturing all the major seaports. The only route for supplies was the Burma Road.

After the fall of Burma, with the Burma Road cut, supplies were airlifted into China by Allied aircraft flying a shuttle service over the lofty mountain ranges between India and China. U.S. officers trained Chinese for future assaults.

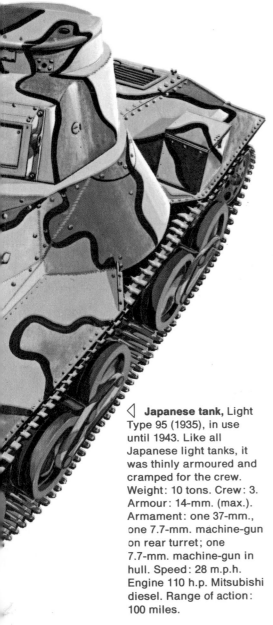

◁ **Japanese tank,** Light Type 95 (1935), in use until 1943. Like all Japanese light tanks, it was thinly armoured and cramped for the crew. Weight: 10 tons. Crew: 3. Armour: 14-mm. (max.). Armament: one 37-mm., one 7.7-mm. machine-gun on rear turret; one 7.7-mm. machine-gun in hull. Speed: 28 m.p.h. Engine 110 h.p. Mitsubishi diesel. Range of action: 100 miles.

△ **A column of Japanese cyclists** on a road through the jungle. Their speed of movement in the Burma campaign surprised the British commanders. "They pressed forward everywhere in almost reckless fashion into the rear of our positions," said one.

El Alamein

△ The "Desert Fox", General Erwin Rommel (left), commander of the German Afrika Korps, became a legend. Friend and foe stood in awe of his skill on the battlefield. **General Bernard Montgomery** (right), known to his troops as "Monty", was admired as a leader who talked (and stood) no nonsense "We'll knock them for six," he said—and he did.

△ **How the 8th Army advanced from El Alamein.** Montgomery refused to launch his offensive until he had massive superiority of men and arms. He said, "Rommel could do what he liked. I had no intention of launching our attack until we were ready." Rommel wrote, "The enemy's superiority is terrific and our resources very small."

"The battle which is now about to begin will be one of the most decisive battles in history. It will be the turning point of the war." The speaker was General Bernard Montgomery, Commander of the British 8th Army.

He was addressing his troops on October 23, 1942. The 8th Army were facing the Axis forces in the Western Desert of North Africa on a line at El Alamein.

Since June–July they had been holding the enemy's drive for Cairo and the Suez Canal. Fortunes in the desert war had fluctuated. After General Wavell had chased the Italians back to Benghazi the German Afrika Korps, under General Rommel, had forced the British to retreat to the border of Egypt. Next General Auchinleck pushed Rommel back to Tobruk but, in May 1942, the Afrika Korps began an attack that was only stopped inside Egypt.

The Battle of Alamein began with a barrage from 1,000 field guns. By the light of the full moon, infantry with fixed bayonets picked their way through enemy minefields clearing two corridors for tanks. In time 1,114 tanks followed, including 300 massive new Shermans from the United States. But the Germans fought back. Rommel threw all his available tanks into a counter-attack. Three days of tank battles followed and neither side advanced.

Then "Monty" launched a new attack. Still the Germans resisted fiercely, but, on November 2, New Zealand troops broke right through the German line. At once tanks rumbled through the gap behind them. Rommel, facing defeat, planned an orderly withdrawal, but Hitler ordered "Stand fast." Next day it was too late. Rommel's forces fled across the desert chased by armoured cars, bombed and machine-gunned by the Desert Air Force. After ten days, the Battle of Alamein was over.

Losses in men and material on both sides were heavy but Rommel's losses were the more severe. He lost most of his tanks and half his men.

△ **Lorries like this German Büssing-NAG 4½-tonner** held the key to victory in the desert for, as Rommel said, supplies were "the basis of the battle." All petrol, ammunition, food and other supplies had to be hauled to the front line. At El Alamein, this was a problem for the Axis forces. Supplies came to them through three seaports, Tripoli (1,420 miles away), Benghazi (660 miles) and Tobruk (370 miles). By contrast, the 8th Army's main depot was at Alexandria, only 70 miles from the front. It had been built up from convoys sailing to Egypt by way of South Africa.

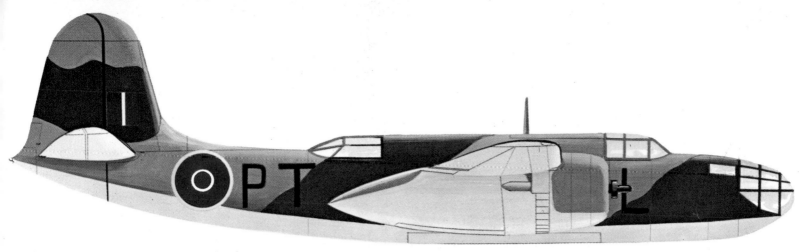

△ **Douglas Boston Mk. III:** twin-engined attack bomber. Speed: 350 m.p.h. at 12,000 ft. Operational range: 1,050 miles. Crew: five. Armament: four fixed machine-guns in nose (two .30, two .50), two .30 machine-guns in turret, one .30 machine-gun in belly. Bomb-load: 1,000 lb. Pattern bombing by these aircraft took an awful toll of the Axis forces before, during and after the Battle of Alamein. With the moon full, they flew missions around the clock.

△ **British artillery at El Alamein, summer 1942 (above left).** On June 25, General Auchinleck took command of an army on the retreat. He lacked the men and materials later available to General Montgomery, having only two infantry divisions and an armoured division not properly organized. But he outmanoeuvred Rommel and finally stopped him.

△ **Sherman tank being unloaded in Egypt.** In 1942 British supplies were being stockpiled in Alexandria, brought by convoys on the long route around South Africa. The new commander of the 8th Army, General Montgomery, was determined not to launch an attack until he had overwhelming superiority in men and materials.

◁ **A German tank surrenders to a British infantryman** in the Battle of Alamein, October 1942. The roaring vehicles churned up the fine sand of the desert so that they were wrapped in dust clouds. Even in October the sun was bright and hot. Men and machines had need of one vital commodity— water.

The Turning Point

Axis territories before 'Barbarossa'

Limit of German advance into Russia Nov. 1942

Projected extent of the 'Greater German Empire' in Russia

△ **This map shows Hitler's dream for an empire** taking in all European Russia. He had even worked out administration plans for the area.

▽ **Soviet soldier waves Red Flag** over battered ruins in Stalingrad. During the fighting, Moscow Radio broadcast a grim reminder: "Every seven seconds a German soldier dies in Russia. 1-2-3-4-5-6-7."

Hitler himself drew up the plans for the campaign in Russia in 1942. The armies facing Leningrad and Moscow were to stand fast. In the south, there was to be a drive to win the rich oilfields of the Caucasus and a thrust eastwards to Stalingrad.

The offensive began on June 10 and all went well. 240,000 Russians were taken prisoner. The first oilfields fell. Farther north, the German 6th Army advanced 275 miles in two months and on August 23 tanks of the 16th Panzer Division rolled into Stalingrad.

For three days the *Luftwaffe* pounded the city from the air until the streets were a chaos of rubble. Then Field-Marshal Friedrich Paulus sent his men forward. To defend Stalingrad, civilians fought beside the Red Army; tanks were driven straight from factories into battle. Street by street, house by house, day and night, an awesome battle began to unfold. It was to last five months.

By November the Germans held nine-tenths of Stalingrad. Then Marshal Zhukov counter-attacked, throwing a circle around the city with the Germans trapped inside. Weeks of horror followed for the Germans. They needed 500 tons of supplies each day, and attempts to provide them by air failed. As the bitter winter closed in they were starving and short of proper clothing. On January 31, 1943, they surrendered. Into captivity went 23 generals, 2,000 officers and 100,000 men.

It was the bloodiest battle of the war, with an estimated half a million men killed *on both sides*. Stalingrad showed the Russians that the Germans were beatable, and afterwards Russian air power was always supreme on the Eastern Front. It was the second turning point of the war.

Meanwhile, the victory at Alamein was being followed up. As Montgomery swept across Libya, Allied forces made landings in Algeria and Morocco. Within three weeks, 180,000 men were landed and the Allies were striking eastwards into Tunisia. Eight days before the end at Stalingrad, "Monty" captured Tripoli and headed for the Tunisian border in the south.

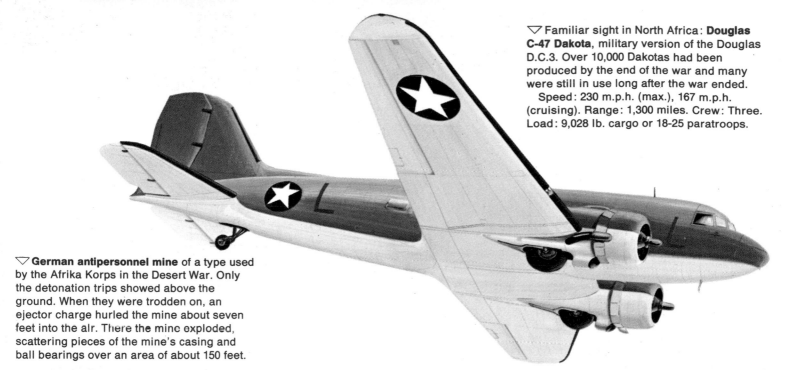

▽ Familiar sight in North Africa: **Douglas C-47 Dakota**, military version of the Douglas D.C.3. Over 10,000 Dakotas had been produced by the end of the war and many were still in use long after the war ended.
  Speed: 230 m.p.h. (max.), 167 m.p.h. (cruising). Range: 1,300 miles. Crew: Three. Load: 9,028 lb. cargo or 18-25 paratroops.

▽ **German antipersonnel mine** of a type used by the Afrika Korps in the Desert War. Only the detonation trips showed above the ground. When they were trodden on, an ejector charge hurled the mine about seven feet into the air. There the mine exploded, scattering pieces of the mine's casing and ball bearings over an area of about 150 feet.

△ **Landings at Algiers, Oran and Casablanca** launched Operation *Torch* on November 8, 1942, and preceded a three-pronged drive to take over Tunisia. Commander-in-Chief was Lt.-Gen. Eisenhower of the U.S. Army. It was the first Allied experience of joint operations by mixed national forces including British, American, and French.
  At the time of the landings, General Montgomery was sweeping across the Libyan Desert. Soon Rommel and the Axis forces in Africa were fighting on two fronts.

△ **British troops watch Americans** in a landing during Operation *Torch*.

35

The Allies Advance

"Before Alamein we never had a victory. After Alamein we never had a defeat."

These words of Winston Churchill are not strictly true. But they emphasize the fact that victory at Alamein, followed so closely by victory at Stalingrad, marked the turning point of the war for the Allies.

From January 1943 the Allies advanced inexorably, and that month Churchill, President Roosevelt and General de Gaulle agreed that the only terms they would offer the Axis were unconditional surrender.

In Africa, Montgomery crossed the Tunisian border and attacked the Mareth Line on March 20, 1943. After six days of hard fighting, the line was broken and Rommel withdrew his remaining forces.

A few days later he flew back to Germany and the Italian Marshal Messe became commander of the Axis forces in Tunisia, now under heavy pressure from the west and the south. The Allies swept forward and on May 7 British troops entered Tunis and Ameri-

cans took the northern port of Bizerta. Five days later, it was all over. 250,415 German and Italian troops surrendered.

On the Russian Front, the spring thaw had brought a lull and Hitler was planning a new offensive, Operation *Citadel*. It opened on July 5 and seven days later 600 German tanks drove into the Russian defences only to come face to face with a similar number of Russian tanks. The greatest tank battle in history followed, lasting eight hours. Then the Germans withdrew. Hitler cancelled Operation *Citadel* and at once the Russians advanced.

On August 23 they took Kharkov, and in September Poltava and Smolensk. Early in October they crossed the River Dnieper and on November 6 liberated Kiev, capital of the Ukraine. The odds were now heavily in favour of the Russians. They had 6 million troops in the field to Germany's 3 million, as well as numerical superiority in tanks, guns and aircraft.

△ **Women in the city of Leningrad,** besieged for 900 days from October 1941. In January 1944, the Red Army drove the Germans back.

△ **Soviet troops** fighting in a railway station on outskirts of Lvov. By capturing the city, the Red Army made a breach in the German defences in the Ukraine. Material from the U.S. helped Russia to turn the tide.

▷ **German troops in Russia** bogged down in mud. The Russians proved to be more mobile in such conditions. In late 1943 the German forces were dwindling. In three months one group lost 133,000 men and only received 33,000 replacements.

△ **Curtiss Kittyhawk,** a fighter plane supplied to the R.A.F. by the U.S., never shone as an interceptor like the Spitfire. But in the 8th Army's drive across North Africa it proved an ideal aircraft for close support of ground forces. Max. speed: 362 m.p.h. Range: 700 miles. Armament: six .50-inch machine-guns, two 250-lb. bombs.

△ **Geography of the end in Tunisia.** U.S. General Eisenhower's 1st Army closed in from the west, "Monty's" 8th Army swept up from the south. On May 12 Eisenhower's second-in-command, General Alexander, sent a joyful cable to Churchill: "The Tunisian campaign is over. All enemy resistance has ceased. We are masters of the North African shores." The Axis Commander-in-Chief had surrendered unconditionally.

◁ **Italian U-boat in the Mediterranean** in the last months of the campaign in North Africa. Benito Mussolini once dreamed of the Mediterranean becoming *Mare Nostrum* (Our Sea) for the Italians. But after the Battle of Cape Matapan his fleet was afraid to put to sea.

With the end in North Africa, control of the Mediterranean assumed a new significance for, before the desert battles were won, the Allies in Africa regarded the campaign as a springboard from which to attack Sicily and Italy. At this stage in the war, it was still a possibility that the ultimate attack on Germany would be made from the south.

△ **May 1943:** Prisoners taken after the surrender of the Axis forces in Tunisia. Their last outpost was on Cape Bon peninsula near Tunis. In moonlight, tanks of 6th Armoured Division overran their positions.

△ **March 1943:** The debris of defeat. Smashed German artillery after the battle of the Mareth Line. Experts regard this as one of "Monty's" most brilliant victories.

The Invasion of Italy

Sicily is a great triangular rock lying just to the south of Italy. It represented a stepping-stone for the invasion of Italy and the Allied forces invaded the island on July 10, 1943.

In 2,700 ships and landing-craft, the U.S. 7th Army and the British 8th Army landed in the south and south-east. The terrain to be covered was difficult and there were twelve Axis divisions defending Sicily. But in 39 days the island was conquered. Allied troops stood on the shores of the Straits of Messina, less than ten miles from Italy.

Meanwhile, the Italians had responded to this danger. Mussolini had been overthrown and imprisoned, and his place taken by Marshal Badoglio, who was ready to make terms with the Allies. The Allies invaded Italy on September 3, landing at Reggio in Calabria. Five days later the Italians surrendered. But Hitler had been ready for this. At once the Germans seized Rome and prepared to defend Italy.

The campaign that followed was long and tough. The U.S. 5th Army landed at Salerno, just south of Naples, and began to fight its way up the west coast.

The British 8th Army, which had swept up from Reggio, now kept to the east. Between them lay a range of mountains—the Apennines.

Rome was captured on June 4, 1944, but it was to be eleven more months before the Allies took all Italy.

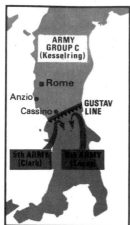
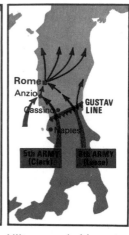

△ **In winter 1943**, the Allies were held up at the newly-built Gustav Line, 70 miles south of Rome. In January the Allies landed behind the line at Anzio, but still the line held. When it fell in May, both armies thrust for Rome, capital of Italy.

▽ **DUKW: six-wheeled amphibious truck**, shown with its splash-board up. The kind of small craft used by the Allies in their landings in Sicily and Italy. Weight: 14,000 lb. Capacity: 25 men or 5,000 lb. cargo. Max. speed: 50 m.p.h. on land, 5.5 knots in water (driven by propeller enclosed in tunnel). Land range: 400 miles at 35 m.p.h. Know-how from these landings aided Allied plans for D-Day.

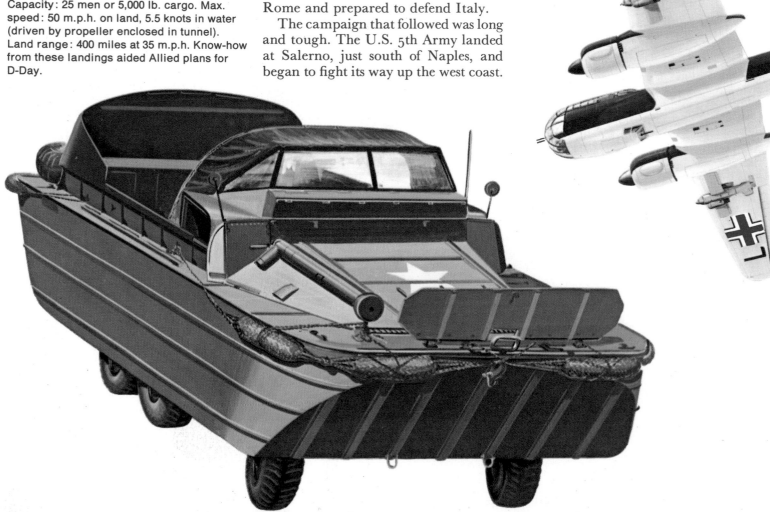

△ **German holed up with heavy machine-gun.** At Monte Cassino, the Germans showed themselves to be adept at using the debris caused by bombing raids or artillery barrages to provide defensive positions. Some experts believe that the pounding given to Monte Cassino hindered rather than aided the Allies.

△ **Dornier Do-217 K3.** Max. speed: 345 m.p.h. Range: 1,550 miles. Crew: 5. Armament: two 7.9 mm. machine guns (nose); two 7.9 mm. (beam mountings); one 13 mm. (dorsal mounting); one 13 mm. (lower rear mounting); four 7.9 mm. (tail cone). Used by the Germans to launch 1,500-lb. glider bombs in the Italian campaign.

△ **The monastery at Monte Cassino,** a key position on the Gustav Line. The monastery stood above the battlefield like a huge look-out post for the Germans and the Allies decided it must be destroyed. On February 14, 1944, leaflets were dropped warning the monks to leave, and the next day 254 bombers dropped 576 tons of bombs, reducing the monastery to rubble (below). In spite of this, new Allied attacks failed. Finally, on May 11, the Allies outflanked Cassino. Six days later Polish troops took Monte Cassino.

▽ **April 1945:** Allied troops advance through typical water-logged country of the Po Valley. This was the final offensive in Italy, shared by the U.S. 5th Army and the British 8th. Its aim was to destroy the German armies south of the Po, to cross the river, and to capture Verona. Verona fell on April 26th and on May 2 the Axis forces in Italy surrendered.

D-Day in Normandy

At 12.15 a.m. on June 6, 1944, 1,333 R.A.F. bombers were dropping 5,000 tons of bombs on coastal batteries in Hitler's Atlantic Wall from the Seine to Cherbourg. D-day had begun.

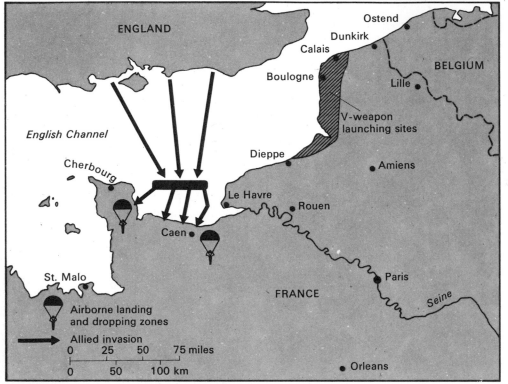

This was the prelude to Operation *Overlord* (the invasion of Europe by the Allies). At the same time, the first airborne troops were landing in Normandy by parachute and glider.

Already the largest fleet ever assembled was in the Channel—5,300 ships and other craft. Over 10,000 planes were ready to join the forthcoming assault by six infantry divisions—3 American, 2 British, 1 Canadian.

Hitler was sure the invaders would be driven back into the sea. But within 48 hours, under a holocaust of German fire, with Allied warships shelling the shore batteries, 107,000 troops and their equipment were landed on the beaches between Caen and Cherbourg.

Less than a month later, 929,000 men and 177,000 vehicles, were on French soil. The Allies were poised to reclaim France and drive on to Germany.

△ **How the Allies returned to Europe on D-day.** When the armada slipped out of the Channel ports on the night of June 5-6, the enemy had no knowledge of the impending invasion. There had been no air reconnaissance during the first five days of June and on June 5-6 naval patrols were cancelled because of bad weather.

△ **U.S. General Dwight D. Eisenhower,** Supreme Commander of the Allied Expeditionary Force that invaded Europe. His orders were to "enter the continent of Europe and with the other United Nations undertake operations aimed at the heart of Germany."

▷ **Liberty ship**—10,000-ton prefabricated cargo vessel assembled in less than five days in the United States. They played a vital part in the Battle of the Atlantic and were in the armada that put to sea for Operation *Overlord*.

The ramps of L.C.I.'s (landing craft, infantry) are down and troops advance to an open beach. Fortunes varied from beach to beach. On the beach code-named *Omaha*, United States troops met the fiercest resistance. But by 4.50 p.m. they had forced their way to a town three-quarters of a mile from the sea. Over the radio in England that evening, King George VI led prayers for the troops in the assault.

△ Obstacles set on the French beaches to tear the bottom out of Allied landing craft— part of Hitler's Atlantic Wall. Also five to six million mines were laid in or near the beaches.

◁ Allied troops landing on the beaches of Normandy on D-day. At first the foreshore was a wilderness of burning vehicles, of shattered craft, of wounded and dead men. But order grew out of the initial chaos and assaults on German strong-points began. By the end of D-day, the Atlantic Wall had been breached for the loss of about 10,000 men killed, wounded or captured.

△ U.S. Army Air Force B-17 Flying Fortress with escorting long-range Mustang fighter. Before D-day and after, Allied bombers pounded the Atlantic Wall in heavy raids.

◁ A great deal of ingenuity went into thinking out ways to make *Overlord* successful. Apart from major items like artificial seaports, improvised docks and an undersea petrol pipeline, there was a wide range of small devices like this one. It is called Bobbin, a Churchill tank chassis fitted out to lay a carpet of canvas 9 ft. 11 in. wide over soft sand. Another device on a Churchill chassis carried a bridge which could be dropped across a 30 ft. gap.

41

Victory in the Pacific

In March 1942 the Japanese invaded New Guinea, a stepping-stone to the invasion of Australia. But the Royal Australian Air Force and the U.S. Air Force held up their advance.

▽ **Australian troops in the New Guinea jungle.** In 1942 men like these stopped the Japanese from capturing Port Moresby—only 350 miles north of Australia. In January 1943, with the Americans, they launched a counter-offensive. But it took more than a year to reclaim New Guinea.

By December, ultimate victory was assured. But the island was not cleared of Japanese until August 1944. Most of the 13,000 Japanese troops fought to the death. Only 38 were taken prisoner. General MacArthur commanded operations on New Guinea.

Also, the southern part of New Guinea around Port Moresby held out. Then came Japan's first defeat—by a U.S. fleet in the Battle of the Coral Sea. It was a new kind of sea-battle fought by aircraft from two opposing fleets. The ships never sighted each other. One U.S. carrier was sunk and another damaged, but the Japanese broke off the fight.

One month later, the Japanese set out to invade Midway in the Hawaiian Islands. On June 3 a U.S. fleet attacked them. This time U.S. dive-bombers sank all four Japanese carriers. The U.S. lost only one carrier. It was a victory as important as the Battle of Alamein. Japan had lost control of the Pacific.

Two months later came the first attack in the long haul to drive back the Japanese. On August 7, 1942, U.S. marines landed on Guadalcanal and other islands in the Solomons. Heavy fighting followed but, in February 1943, the Japanese withdrew and the U.S. advance began.

By October 1944, U.S. forces were ready to invade the Philippine Islands. A Japanese fleet put out to drive them back. The two fleets, with 166 U.S. and 25 Japanese warships, met on October 23 in the Battle of Leyte Gulf. 1,280 U.S. and 716 Japanese aircraft were also used in the largest sea-air battle ever fought. It lasted three days. Japanese *kamikaze* pilots deliberately crashed their planes on U.S. ships. Yet again the Americans won. The Japanese lost 4 carriers, 2 battleships, 8 cruisers and several destroyers. The Americans lost only 3 cruisers and 3 destroyers.

By February 24, 1945, U.S. forces had recaptured Manila, and MacArthur was planning the invasion of Japan itself.

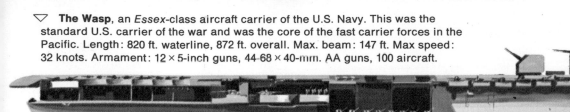

▽ **The Wasp,** an *Essex*-class aircraft carrier of the U.S. Navy. This was the standard U.S. carrier of the war and was the core of the fast carrier forces in the Pacific. Length: 820 ft. waterline, 872 ft. overall. Max. beam: 147 ft. Max speed: 32 knots. Armament: 12 × 5-inch guns, 44-68 × 40-mm. AA guns, 100 aircraft.

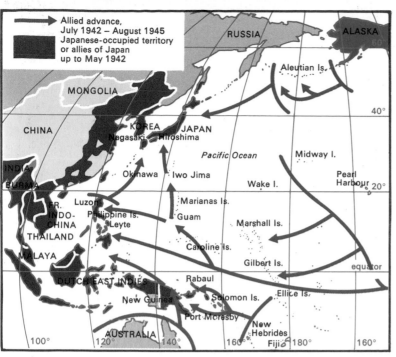

△ **U.S. troops make a landing** on an enemy beach. The Americans produced an entire new range of landing craft.

◁ **This map shows how the Allies advanced across the Pacific.** The pattern of attack was: **1** Strikes by carrier-based aircraft. **2** Bombardment by warships; transports, cargo ships move in. **3** Landings.

▷ **Cross-section view of *Essex*-class carrier** with reinforced armour at and below water-line; oil storage tanks clear of danger spots.

Key:
1 Lift.
2 20- and 40-mm. AA guns.
3 Stacked lifeboats.
4 Fan motors.
5 Airframe workshop.
6 Workshop deck and lift machinery.
7 Ammo and aircraft stores.
8 Air-conditioning plants.
9 Main hanger.
10 AA guns.
11 AA guns.
12 Servicing hangar.
13 Aero engine stores.
14 Engine servicing shop.
15 Port ammo stores.
16 Emergency lighting plant.
17 Engine-cooling motor.
18 Steam pipes to turbines.
19 Turbines.
20 Fireproof coffer dam.
21 Aviation spirit tank.
22 Oil fuel tanks.

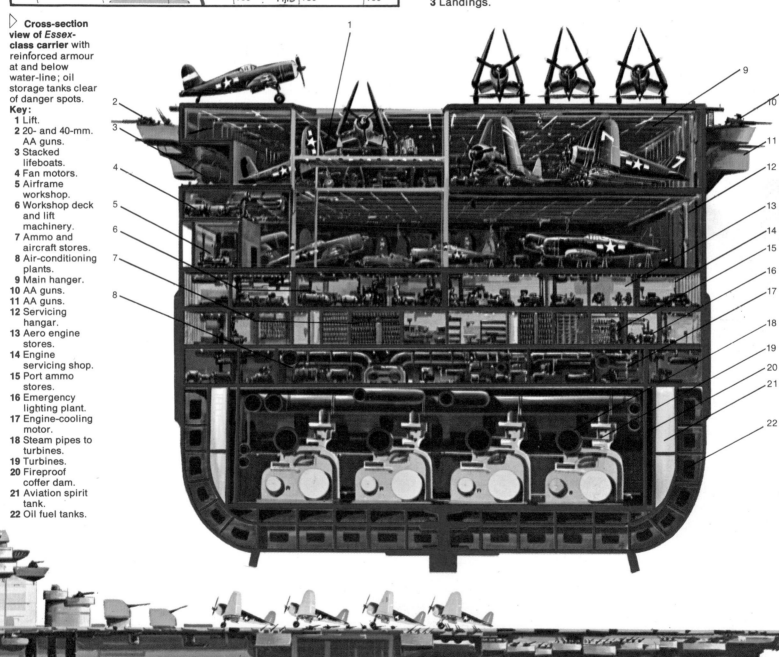

The Final Defeats

▽ **The spirit that took the Red Army to Berlin.** "Death to the German invaders!" says this Soviet poster.

▽ **American column** delayed while moving up to meet the German assault in the Ardennes, December 1944. Hitler's counter-offensive meant using troops badly needed on the Eastern Front.

On July 1, 1944, Field Marshal Karl von Runstedt, Supreme Commander of the German armies in France, reported by telephone to one of the top Nazis in Berlin that the latest German counter-attacks on the Allied invasion forces had failed.

"What shall we do?" he was asked. He replied, "Make peace, you fools. What else can you do?" Already it was clear to him that Germany was doomed. In ten weeks after D-day the Allies destroyed the German 7th Army, and by August 25 Paris was liberated.

By September the Germans had fallen back to the Siegfried Line on their own border. In a bold attempt to outflank the Line, the Allies launched an airborne assault in Holland. But the airborne troops were defeated at Arnhem and the advance came to a halt.

In December-January, the Germans used their last reserves in a counter-attack in the Ardennes (Belgium), known as the Battle of the Bulge, which the Allies won with heavy losses on both sides. The scene was set for the final act, the conquest of Germany.

On the Eastern Front, the Russians had opened a new offensive on January 13, and five days later entered Warsaw, capital of Poland. By the end of the month, the Red Army was on the River Oder in Germany, less than 100 miles from Berlin. In February, Allied troops entered Germany in the west.

On March 22-23 U.S. General Patton and General Montgomery crossed the Rhine in two different places and led their armies into the heart of Germany. Meanwhile the Russians liberated Vienna, capital of Austria, and Prague, capital of Czechoslovakia. Even Hitler now knew Germany was doomed to defeat, but he refused to ask for terms.

The advances from east and west went on until, on April 27, Russian and American forces met. On May 2, Berlin was captured. One day earlier Hitler had killed himself. Six days later Germany surrendered.

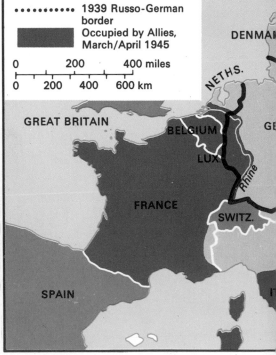

•••••••••• 1939 Russo-German border

▨ Occupied by Allies, March/April 1945

0   200   400 miles
0   200   400   600 km

DENMARK

NETHS.

GREAT BRITAIN

BELGIUM

LUX.

FRANCE

Rhine

SWITZ.

SPAIN

△ **The strategic situation in March/April 1945**—the ring around Germany closing in. By this time German soldiers hardly knew what was happening. Air cover was non-

△ **Craft like this amphibious Buffalo** were used by Montgomery's army to cross the River Rhine, a formidable water barrier.

◁ **Soviet soldier on top of the Reichstag** in Berlin, May 1945. The Russian General Koniev said, "Think of what Berlin meant to us, and imagine the passionate desire of us all, from general to private, to see Berlin, this lair of the Nazis, and take it by storm." The Soviet drive to Berlin was begun on the River Oder on April 16-17 and it took the Russians six days of bitter fighting to smash their way 30 miles to the outskirts of the city.

△ **Historic scene** which brought the end of World War Two in Europe in sight. U.S. G.I. meets Russian soldier in the heart of Germany.

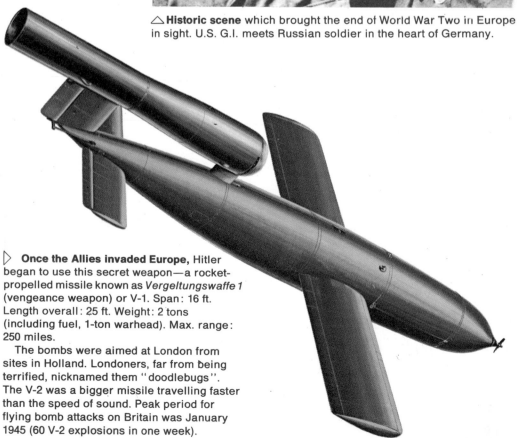

▷ **Once the Allies invaded Europe,** Hitler began to use this secret weapon—a rocket-propelled missile known as *Vergeltungswaffe 1* (vengeance weapon) or V-1. Span: 16 ft. Length overall: 25 ft. Weight: 2 tons (including fuel, 1-ton warhead). Max. range: 250 miles.

The bombs were aimed at London from sites in Holland. Londoners, far from being terrified, nicknamed them "doodlebugs". The V-2 was a bigger missile travelling faster than the speed of sound. Peak period for flying bomb attacks on Britain was January 1945 (60 V-2 explosions in one week).

existent, communications were breaking down. Some units were left for days on end without orders. The knowledge of ultimate defeat was spreading throughout the ranks.

Japan Fights to the Death

Okinawa is an island lying 400 miles to the south of Japan. In 1945 the United States, planning the ultimate invasion of Japan, believed that they needed to capture Okinawa first.

⇕ **Japanese suicide pilot,** known as a *kamikaze*, scores a hit on a U.S. aircraft carrier. The Japanese believed in absolute obedience to their Emperor and they were ready to sacrifice their lives for him and the Japanese nation.

Medium-bombers could raid Japan from the island and it was estimated that 780 aircraft could be based there. Operation *Iceberg*, the assault on Okinawa, began on April 1, 1945, when the greatest armada in naval history sailed into Japanese waters. It consisted of more than 40 aircraft carriers, 18 battleships, 200 destroyers, hundreds of cruisers, supply ships, mine-sweepers, gunboats, landing craft, patrol boats, salvage ships, repair ships and submarines as well as 1,500 transports carrying 182,000 troops.

The first landings were made on Okinawa on April 6 with little opposition. The Japanese proposed to defeat the invaders at a well-prepared position, the Shuri Line. At the same time, they intended to destroy the American armada now spread out in the East China Sea around Okinawa.

To do this they were depending on air strikes including attacks by bomb-laden planes flown by suicide pilots who crashed on their targets. Some naval attacks were made, by surface craft and

submarines. But there was an element of despair about these.

When the *Yamato*, the largest battleship in the world, sailed into action, she only had enough fuel for a one-way voyage and she was promptly sunk. But massed air attacks left their mark on the U.S. armada. From April 6 to June 22 more than 3,000 suicide attacks alone were made on the U.S. ships, sinking 21 and damaging 66.

In a typical incident on April 16, the destroyer *Laffey* was attacked by 50 aircraft. Six suicide pilots crashed on her. But she shot down nine aircraft and survived, badly damaged, with 31 crew dead, 72 wounded.

The battle for Okinawa was won on June 22, when the Japanese Commander-in-Chief committed suicide. But the final assault on Japan did not follow. Instead, on August 6, the first atomic bomb was dropped on Hiroshima. When the Japanese refused to surrender, a second atomic bomb was dropped on Nagasaki on August 9. Five days later, Japan gave in.

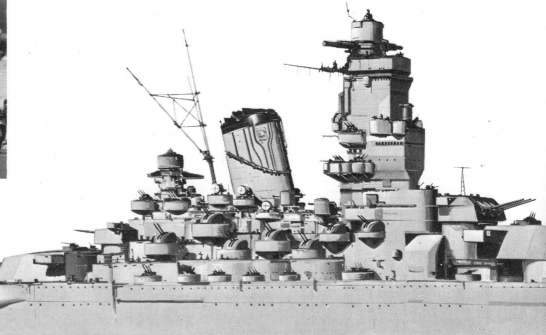

△ **Devastation at Hiroshima.** At 17.19 on August 6, 1945, four B 29s of the U.S. Army Air Force and one Superfortress, *Enola Gay* appeared in the cloudless sky over Hiroshima, seventh largest city in Japan. The Superfortress released a single bomb which descended five miles by parachute and burst over the target. It was the first atomic bomb to be used in war. President Roosevelt had died some months earlier, and the decision to use this new, terrible weapon was made by the new President, Harry S. Truman.

▽ **The *Yamato*** remains the largest battleship ever built. Length: 863 ft. Beam: 127 ft. Full-load displacement: 72,809 tons. Had nine 18-inch guns 75 ft. long and weighing 162 tons.

She sailed into the Okinawa battle zone with one light cruiser and eight destroyers but no air cover. At 08.23 on April 7 she was spotted by a U.S. plane and from that moment her fate was sealed. The first attack came at 12.32 and she was a floating wreck, hit by five bombs and ten torpedoes, when, at 14.32, she sank with 2,488 men of her crew of 2,767. The light cruiser and four of the destroyers went down with her. Japan now had only one battleship left, the *Haruna*.

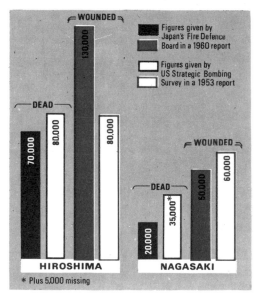

△ **Estimates of the casualties** that occurred in the devastation of Hiroshima vary enormously. In 1960 the U.S. Casualty Commission gave a figure of 79,400, but the Hiroshima Peace Memorial Museum gives a figure of 240,000 people killed in the bombing or dying afterwards from radiation sickness. These figures compare with about 168,000 killed in the world's worst conventional air raid—on Tokio on March 9-10, 1945.

△ **Japanese surrender in Burma.** The Allies counter-attacked in 1943 but the fight was long and hard. In 1944, the Japanese were again on the borders of India at Imphal. But in 1945 the tide turned for the Allies. In the north, combined United States and Chinese forces drove southwards and then eastwards to link up with Chinese driving west from southern China. In the south the British 14th Army took the capital, Mandalay, and drove on for the great port of Rangoon. Rangoon fell on May 3 and, after that, only mopping-up operations remained.

Why War Began...

World War II occurred, basically, because Germany and Japan wanted to expand.

Italy had similar but more modest aims and Mussolini, the dictator of Italy, might never, acting alone, have precipitated a large-scale international conflict.

It has been said that the seeds of World War Two were sown in the Treaty of Versailles at the end of World War One. Certainly Germany constantly expressed resentment at many of the terms of the Treaty, particularly the so-called "War Guilt Clause", by which Germany was forced to acknowledge her responsibility for causing the war.

Germany also felt bitter over the amount of money she was supposed to pay in reparations to the Allies, though, in fact, she never paid the enormous sums which France, in particular, demanded. Resentful over lost national pride and the poor financial state to which Germany had been reduced by the Great Depression of 1929, the people were ready to accept the violent leadership of Adolf Hitler, founder of the National Socialist or Nazi party.

In addition there was the failure of the League of Nations, founded after World War One to preserve the peace of the world. President Woodrow Wilson of the United States was one of the architects of the League. When he failed to persuade his own country to become a member, he warned that World War One would have to be fought all over again—and perhaps he was right.

The rise of Japan

In the East, Japan, although on the side of the victors in World War One and a member of the League of Nations, was dissatisfied with her lot. A country of islands with few natural resources, Japan sought to extend her territory on the mainland of Asia, and, in 1931, overran Manchuria which, at that time, was being taken over by China.

The League of Nations considered this action and condemned it but Japan did not withdraw her troops. Instead, in 1933, she resigned from the League and in 1937 she embarked upon the conquest of China. This war later became part of the international struggle called World War Two, although, in the West, the War is regarded as having begun on September 3, 1939.

German expansion

Meanwhile, in Germany, Hitler was pressing forward his plans for a new German empire in the east. The Germans wanted *lebensraum* (living-space) and the plains of Poland and the hills of Czechoslovakia would provide it.

By 1936, Germany as well as Japan had resigned from the League of Nations and so had Italy, Mussolini having invaded and conquered Ethiopia while the League looked on powerless.

In 1936, Germany and Italy made an agreement known as the "Axis Pact". By this time, Germany had been excused the payment of further reparations and Hitler was re-arming openly. The statesmen of Britain and France, feeling perhaps that the Germans had been harshly treated, were striving to accommodate Hitler's demands. They had set the stage for Germany's acts of aggression and the ultimate tragedy of another world war.

The Main Events 1939-1945

△ **March 1938: Hitler rides in triumph** through Vienna, arm extended in the Nazi salute. His troops had entered Austria and he had declared an *anschluss*—union of Germany and Austria.

△ **At Antwerp in 1944, this ten-year-old was captured.** As the war went on, the age of call-up on both sides fell lower. With her back to the wall, Germany enrolled youths into the armed forces.

△ **Help for civilian victim of Allied air raid** on Mannheim, Germany, 1944. In World War Two, civilians knew the horror of war, including the ultimate horror of Hiroshima.

1939

15 Mar	German troops march into Prague, take over Bohemia, Moravia.
16 Mar	Hitler declares: "Czechoslovakia has ceased to exist."
23 Mar	Poland rejects German proposals for Danzig.
7 Apr	Italy annexes Albania.
26 Apr	Men aged 20-21 to be called into armed forces in Britain.
22 May	Germany forms military alliance with Italy; called the "Pact of Steel".
23 Aug	Germany signs non-aggression pact with Russia; secret clauses share Poland.
26-31 Aug	Chamberlain, Daladier in talks with Hitler. Talks fail.
31 Aug	Women, children evacuated from London to "safe areas" outside towns.
1 Sept	Poland invaded. France, Britain demand withdrawal of German troops.
2 Sept	Chamberlain sends ultimatum to Hitler.
3 Sept	Britain declares war on Germany. France, Australia, New Zealand follow suit. S.S. *Athenia* sunk by U-boat.
6 Sept	South Africa declares war on Germany.
10 Sept	Canada declares war on Germany.
17 Sept	Soviet Union invades Poland.
27 Sept	Warsaw surrenders.
29 Sept	German-Soviet treaty splits up Poland between them.
3 Oct	British Expeditionary Force on Belgian Frontier.
6 Oct	Last Polish troops cease fighting.
30 Nov	Soviet Union invades Finland.

1940

13 Mar	Treaty of Moscow ends Soviet-Finnish war.
29 Mar	Soviet Union announces neutrality.
9 Apr	German troops occupy Denmark, invade Norway.
13 Apr	Battle of Narvik. Seven German destroyers sunk by Allies.
10 May	Germany attacks Holland, Belgium, Luxembourg. Chamberlain resigns. Churchill new Prime Minister of Britain.
15 May	Holland surrenders to Germany.
20 May	German tanks reach English Channel.
25 May	Allies surrounded on Channel coast.
26 May	Operation *Dynamo*—evacuation of Allied troops from Dunkirk begins.
27 May	Belgian Army surrenders to Germans.
3 June	Dunkirk evacuation ends.
10 June	Italy declares war on Britain and France. Canada declares war on Italy. Norway surrenders to Germans.
14 June	Germans enter Paris.
16 June	Pétain becomes Premier of France.
17 June	Pétain asks Germans for peace terms.
18 June	De Gaulle broadcasts from London for "Free France".
22 June	France-Italy armistice signed.
25 June	Fighting ends in France.
10 July	Battle of Britain begins.
16 July	Operation *Sealion*, invasion of Britain, planned for mid-August.
19 Aug	British withdraw from Somaliland.
23 Aug	All-night raid on London—start of the "Blitz".
17 Sept	Hitler postpones *Sealion*.
27 Sept	Germany, Italy, Japan sign pact. *Luftwaffe* lose 55 aircraft over Britain.
7 Oct	German troops enter Rumania.
28 Oct	Italians invade Greece.
9 Dec	British offensive in Western Desert begins.

1941

12 Feb	General Rommel arrives Tripoli.
1 Mar	Bulgaria joins Axis.
24 Mar	British Somaliland cleared of Italians.
25 Mar	Yugoslavia signs pact with Germany.
27 Mar	Revolution in Yugoslavia.
28 Mar	Battle of Cape Matapan.
3 Apr	Rommel launches offensive.
6 Apr	Germans invade Greece, Yugoslavia.
21 Apr	Greek Army gives in to Germans. British forces begin evacuation.
20 May	German attack on Crete begins.
24 May	*Hood, Prince of Wales* engage *Bismarck, Prinz Eugen. Hood* sunk.
27 May	*Bismarck* sunk.
1 June	British evacuate Crete.
22 June	Germany invades Russia.
4 July	Tito announces resistance to Germans in Yugoslavia.
15 July	Germans capture Smolensk.
19 Sept	Germans capture Kiev, Poltava.
26 Sept	Hitler orders winter offensive against Moscow.
2 Oct	Fierce German attack on Moscow.
24 Oct	Germans take Kharkov.
27 Oct	Russians under Zhukov counter-attack in Moscow area.
29 Oct	German break-through in Crimea.
18 Nov	New Western Desert Campaign by British 8th Army begins.
25 Nov	New German attack on Moscow.
26 Nov	German armour stopped 19 miles from Moscow.
5 Dec	Hitler abandons Moscow offensive for winter.
7 Dec	Japanese attack U.S. Naval base at Pearl Harbour.
8 Dec	Allies, United States declare war on Japan. Russia remains neutral.
15 Dec	British withdraw in Malaya, Burma, Kowloon.
25 Dec	Hong Kong surrenders to Japanese.

1942

2 Jan	Japanese occupy Manila.
16 Jan	Japanese invade Burma from Thailand.
21 Jan	Rommel starts new offensive in Libya.
28 Jan	Russians advance into Ukraine.
5 Feb	Rommel stopped at Gazala.
15 Feb	Singapore surrenders to Japanese.
22 Feb	General MacArthur leaves the Philippines.
27 Feb	Battle of the Java Sea.
1 Mar	Russian offensive in Crimea.
8 Mar	Japanese enter Rangoon.
1 Apr	Japanese landings on Dutch New Guinea.
9 Apr	U.S. troops on Bataan surrender.
30 Apr	Japanese complete conquest of Burma.
6 May	U.S. troops on Corregidor surrender.
7-8 May	Battle of Coral Sea.
11 May	Japanese launch new offensives in China.
15 May	Retreating British cross Burma-India Frontier.
17 May	Germans halt Russian offensive east of Kharkov.
30 May	First 1,000-bomber raid by R.A.F. on Cologne.
4 June	Battle of Midway.
19 June	Churchill, Roosevelt meet in U.S.
30 June	Rommel advances to El Alamein.
31 July	Germans cross River Don.
7 Aug	U.S. Marines land on Guadalcanal.
13 Aug	Montgomery takes command of British 8th Army in Middle East.
19 Aug	German 6th Army begins attack on Stalingrad.
16 Sept	Germans enter Stalingrad.
11 Oct	Battle of Cape Esperance off Guadalcanal.
23 Oct	Battle of Alamein begins.
4 Nov	Axis retreat from El Alamein.
8 Nov	Operation *Torch*, the invasion of North-West Africa, begins.
25 Nov	British 8th Army occupies Sirte.

1943

3 Jan	Germans start withdrawal from Caucasus.
4 Jan	Japanese begin to evacuate Guadalcanal.
18 Jan	Russians attack, end siege of Leningrad.
23 Jan	British 8th Army enters Tripoli.
27 Jan	U.S.A.F.'s first raid on Germany. Target Wilhelmshaven.
31 Jan	Paulus surrenders German 6th Army at Stalingrad.
8 Feb	Russians recapture Kursk.
16 Feb	Russians recapture Kharkov.
17 Feb	British 8th Army captures Medenin.
6 Mar	Rommel leaves Afrika Korps.
15 Mar	Germans recapture Kharkov.
20 Mar	British 8th Army attacks Mareth Line.
28 Mar	8th Army takes Mareth.
29 Mar	8th Army takes Gabes, El Hamma.
7 Apr	8th Army links up with U.S. II Corps.
7 May	Allies overrun Tunis and Bizerta.
13 May	Axis forces in North Africa surrender.
17 May	"Dam Busters" raid by R.A.F.
27 May	British mission parachutes to Tito's Partisans.
5 July	Germans' last offensive on Eastern Front near Kursk.
10 July	Invasion of Sicily begins.
12 July	Germans lose "greatest tank battle in history"; Russian counter-offensive begins.
25 July	Mussolini arrested; Badoglio forms new Italian government.
17 Aug	Axis resistance in Sicily ends.
23 Aug	Russians recapture Kharkov.
3 Sept	Germans occupy Rome.
12 Sept	Mussolini rescued by Germans.
25 Sept	Russians recapture Smolensk.
1 Oct	Allies capture Naples.
6 Nov	Russians recapture Kiev.

1944

5 Jan	Allies attack in Italy east of Cassino.
22 Jan	Allied landings at Anzio, north of Cassino.
31 Jan	U.S. troops invade Marshall Islands.
4 Feb	Japanese offensive in Burma.
10 Apr	Russians recapture Odessa.
5 May	British 14th Army attacks Assam.
9 May	Sebastopol recaptured by Russians.
13 May	Allies break through Gustav Line on way to Rome.
18 May	Poles capture Monte Cassino.
4 June	Allies enter Rome.
6 June	D-day. Allies invade Normandy.
15 June	U.S. troops land on Saipan.
27 June	Russians cross River Dnieper.
29 June	Cherbourg captured by Allies.
16 July	Allies in Italy reach R. Arno.
17 July	Russians enter Poland.
20 July	"July Bomb Plot": attempt to kill Hitler.
21 July	U.S. Marines land on Guam.
25 Aug	Allies liberate Paris.
29 Aug	French troops cross Rhône.
30 Aug	Russians take Ploesti, Rumania.
3 Sept	British liberate Brussels.
4 Sept	British liberate Antwerp.
12 Sept	U.S. 1st Army crosses German frontier near Aachen.
17-19 Sept	Operation *Market Garden*: Allied airborne attack on Arnhem fails.
24 Sept	British 2nd Army reaches Rhine.
1 Oct	Russians enter Yugoslavia.
14 Oct	British liberate Athens.
20 Oct	U.S. 6th Army invades Leyte.
23 Oct	Russians enter East Prussia.
23-26 Oct	Battle of Leyte Gulf.
18 Nov	U.S. 3rd Army crosses German frontier.
15 Dec	Chinese capture Bhamo in Burma.
16 Dec	"Battle of Bulge" begins.

1945

11 Jan	Russians enter Warsaw.
22 Jan	Burma road re-opened.
28 Jan	"Battle of Bulge" ends.
1 Feb	U.S. 7th Army reaches Siegfried Line.
6 Feb	Russians cross Upper Oder.
19 Feb	U.S. Marines land on Iwo Jima.
24 Feb	U.S. troops reclaim Manila.
7 Mar	U.S. 1st Army crosses Rhine.
20 Mar	British 14th Army captures Mandalay, Burma.
23 Mar	British, Canadians cross Rhine.
30 Mar	Russians capture Danzig.
1 Apr	U.S. 1st and 9th Armies encircle Ruhr.
6 Apr	U.S. troops invade Okinawa. Battle of East China Sea in progress.
7 Apr	Russians enter Vienna.
10 Apr	U.S. 9th Army takes Hanover.
12 Apr	President Roosevelt dies; new president Harry S. Truman.
13 Apr	Russians occupy Vienna.
15 Apr	Canadians reach sea in North Holland.
20 Apr	U.S. 7th Army captures Nuremberg.
21 Apr	In Italy, Allies enter Bologna.
23 Apr	Russians reach Berlin. Italy: Allies reach River Po.
25 Apr	U.S. 1st Army patrols meet Soviet troops.
28 Apr	Mussolini captured, killed by Italian partisans.
29 Apr	Allies near Trieste (Italy). German forces in Italy sign surrender for 2 May. U.S. 7th Army in Munich.
30 Apr	Hitler kills himself.
2 May	Russians complete capture of Berlin.
3 May	British 14th Army captures Rangoon, Burma.
7 May	Germans sign unconditional surrender.
6 Aug	Atomic bomb dropped on Hiroshima.
9 Aug	Atomic bomb dropped on Nagasaki.
14 Aug	Japan agrees to unconditional surrender.

The Results of the War

△ **Sir Alexander Fleming,** discoverer of the so-called "wonder drug" penicillin, which saved the lives of countless soldiers, sailors and airmen in World War Two. Manufacture of penicillin began in 1944.

The document that formally concluded World War Two in Europe was signed at Rheims, France, on May 7, 1945.

In the Pacific, the surrender of the Japanese was signed aboard the United States battleship *Missouri*, anchored in Tokio Bay, on September 2, 1945.

World War Two took the lives of more people than any other war in history. Estimates of the casualties vary considerably, the figure for the total of war dead, civilian and military, ranging upwards from 22 million. The Guinness Book of Records states: "The total number of fatalities, including battle deaths and civilians of all countries, is estimated to have been 54,800,000." This includes almost six million Jews who were put to death by the Germans or died in the concentration camps and over four million Poles who died as a result of war or persecution.

According to some estimates, the Soviet Union lost 20 million military and civilian dead. As to the cost of the war, The Guinness Book of Records states: "It is certain that the material cost of World War Two far transcended that of the rest of history's wars *put together*. In the case of Britain, the cost of £34,423 million was over five times as great as that of World War One. The total cost to the Soviet Union was estimated as 2,500,000,000,000 roubles (£100,000 million)."

For six years death and destruction raged on a world-wide scale. Whole cities and vast stretches of countryside were laid waste and many beautiful and historic buildings and their contents were destroyed.

On the other hand, World War Two hastened progress in a number of spheres. It produced new antibiotic drugs like penicillin. It hastened the development of the jet aeroplane, and produced radar. It provided the scientific basis of rocketry that was soon to take man to the Moon while the atomic bomb, that awesome weapon, had peaceful connotations in the development of nuclear power.

△ **Germans collect milk ration.** The aftermath of the war in Germany—poverty, hunger, unemployment. Only 40 per cent of the food needed to feed her population was available. Rationing would go on.

△ **Gloster E28/39**—"Flying Tea Kettle"—Sir Frank Whittle's original jet aircraft made its first flight on May 15, 1941, and the Gloster Meteor jet fighter went into service in 1944. At first, people stared in wonder at planes without propellers.

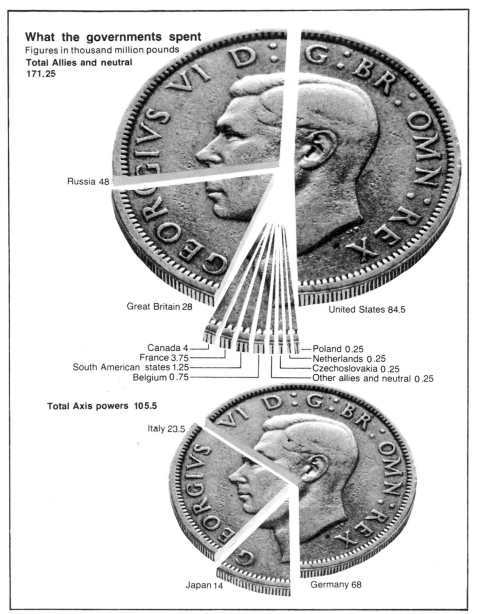

What the governments spent
Figures in thousand million pounds
Total Allies and neutral 171.25

Russia 48

Great Britain 28

United States 84.5

Canada 4
France 3.75
South American states 1.25
Belgium 0.75

Poland 0.25
Netherlands 0.25
Czechoslovakia 0.25
Other allies and neutral 0.25

Total Axis powers 105.5

Italy 23.5

Japan 14

Germany 68

△ **Estimates of what the war cost** to the various governments vary enormously. The estimates on which this diagram are based are not exaggerated.

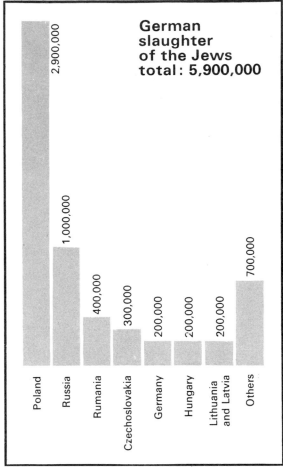

German slaughter of the Jews total: 5,900,000

Poland	2,900,000
Russia	1,000,000
Rumania	400,000
Czechoslovakia	300,000
Germany	200,000
Hungary	200,000
Lithuania and Latvia	200,000
Others	700,000

△ **These grim statistics** underline one of the most hideous aspects of Hitler's régime in Germany--the persecution of the Jews which was extended to whatever countries the Germans took over in their years of expansion. In 1935, laws were passed discriminating against the Jews and in 1938 violent attacks on Jews began. When World War Two started, the Germans began the systematic extermination of Jews in gas chambers and concentration camps.

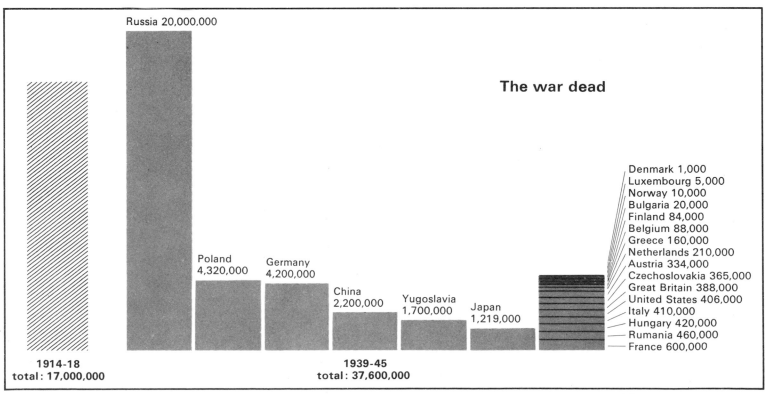

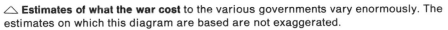

The war dead

Russia 20,000,000

Poland 4,320,000

Germany 4,200,000

China 2,200,000

Yugoslavia 1,700,000

Japan 1,219,000

Denmark 1,000
Luxembourg 5,000
Norway 10,000
Bulgaria 20,000
Finland 84,000
Belgium 88,000
Greece 160,000
Netherlands 210,000
Austria 334,000
Czechoslovakia 365,000
Great Britain 388,000
United States 406,000
Italy 410,000
Hungary 420,000
Rumania 460,000
France 600,000

1914-18 total: 17,000,000

1939-45 total: 37,600,000

△ **The figures for war dead,** military and civilian, on which this diagram is based, fall between the extreme estimated figures.

Who's Who

Chamberlain

Churchill

Giraud

Goering

Attlee, Clement Richard, 1st Earl Attlee (1883-1967), Prime Minister of Britain 1945-51, took Churchill's place at Potsdam conference with Stalin and Truman.

Chamberlain, Neville (1869-1940), British Prime Minister 1937-40. A popular hero on his return from Munich in 1938 with hope of "peace in our time"; forced to resign after the Allied campaign failed in Norway, 1940.

Chiang Kai-shek (1887-   ), Chinese general and statesman, leader of the country from 1926 to 1949. Driven out by the Communists, founded Nationalist China on island of Taiwan (Formosa).

Churchill, Sir Winston Spencer (1874-1965), Prime Minister of Britain 1940-45. When he took office he announced, "I have nothing to offer but blood, toil, tears and sweat." His defiant speeches (broadcast on the radio) and courageous example made him an inspiring war-leader, though the Service chiefs often found him a difficult taskmaster. P.M. again 1951-55, he retired at 80 and was knighted.

Eden, Anthony, Earl of Avon (1897-   ), British statesman. Foreign Secretary 1935-38, he resigned in protest against the policy of appeasing (giving in) to Hitler advocated by Chamberlain. Foreign Secretary 1940-45, 1951-55. Prime Minister 1955-57.

Eisenhower

de Gaulle

Eisenhower, Dwight D. (1898-1969), American general, commanded the Allied forces which invaded North Africa in 1942 (Operation *Torch*); Supreme Commander of the Allied Forces in Europe 1944-45 including D-day. President of the United States 1953-61.

de Gaulle, Charles André Joseph Marie (1890-1971), general and leader of the Free French after the fall of France in 1940. Was among the first to enter liberated Paris (1944). Helped France to begin rebuilding after the war but retired in 1946. Recalled as President 1958-69.

Giraud, Henri (1879-1949), French general captured by Germans in 1940. Escaped in 1942 and became deputy to de Gaulle as Free French leader.

Goering, Hermann (1893-1946), German fighter ace in World War One, supreme commander of the *Luftwaffe* in World War Two. Tried for war crimes and sentenced to death, he killed himself.

Harris, Sir Arthur (1892-   ), C.-in-C. British Bomber Command in World War Two. Known as "Bomber Harris", he believed in mass raids and area bombing.

Hess, Rudolf (1894-   ), German statesman, one of the top Nazis. Incredibly flew alone to Scotland in 1941 on the eve of the invasion of Russia to try to persuade Britain to make peace with Germany. Was imprisoned in the Tower of London. Condemned at Nuremberg to life imprisonment.

Hirohito   Hitler

Hirohito (1901-   ), emperor of Japan from 1926, saw the rise of militarism which ended in the disaster of World War Two. Afterwards, under United States occupation, became a democratic ruler.

Hitler, Adolf (1889-1945). An Austrian corporal who won the Iron Cross in World War One, Hitler afterwards started the National Socialist German Workers' Party (the Nazis) and became Chancellor of Germany in 1933. With the power of a dictator, he began to persecute Jews and expand the boundaries of Germany. He was hiding in an air raid shelter when Russian armies reached Berlin and is believed to have killed himself.

Kesselring, Albert (1885-1960), German general. A former *Luftwaffe* commander, became C.-in-C. in Italy in 1943. In March 1945 he took over from Runstedt as C.-in-C. on the Western Front. Tried in 1947 as a war criminal. At first condemned to death, then to life imprisonment and released in 1952.

Kesselring

Mannerheim

De Lattre de Tassigny, Jean (1889-1952), Marshal of France. Sent by Vichy government to command in Tunisia, he was recalled for sympathizing with Allies; escaped in 1943 to London. Subsequently a leader of the Free French, taking part in the liberation of France 1944-45.

Leclerc, Jacques Philippe (1902-47), Marshal of France. Led Free French force from Lake Chad across the Sahara Desert to join the Allies in North Africa. Liberated Paris 1944.

MacArthur   Montgomery

MacArthur, Douglas (1880-1964), American general, commanding U.S. armed forces in Asia when the Japanese attacked Pearl Harbour. He planned and executed the recovery of the islands lost to the Japanese and in 1945 returned to the Philippines. Received the Japanese surrender on board the *Missouri* on September 2, 1945. At war's end, he was sole administrator of the military government in Japan.

Mannerheim, Baron Carl (1867-1951), field marshal, Finnish soldier and statesman. Fought with the Russian Army against Japan in 1904-5 and in World War One. Commanded the Finns against the Russians in 1939-40. President of Finnish Republic 1944-46.

Mao Tse-tung (1893-   ), leader of Chinese Communist guerillas fighting against the Japanese in World War Two. In 1949 drove Chiang Kai-shek out of China and started the People's Republic of China as Chairman of the Chinese Communist Party.

Marshall, George Catlett (1880-1959), American soldier and statesman, Chief of Staff of the U.S. Army 1939-45. Initiated "Marshall Plan" for Europe under which the United States agreed to send aid to Europe. Official name: European Recovery Programme. It went on to 1951.

Montgomery, Bernard, Viscount Montgomery of Alamein (1887-   ), British field marshal. As commander of the 8th Army in North Africa decisively defeated the Axis forces at Alamein, October 1942, the "turning point of the war." Led the 8th Army in the invasion of Sicily and Italy. Led the British invasion forces on D-day being C.-in-C. British Forces in France and Germany 1944-46.

Mountbatten, Louis, 1st Earl Mountbatten of Burma (1900-   ), British admiral. In 1942 he was made Chief of Combined Operations. Appointed Supreme Allied Commander in South-East Asia, 1945, he saw the reconquest of Burma and accepted the surrender of the Japanese.

Mussolini, Benito (1883-1945), dictator of Italy. Rose to power in the 1920's as head of the Fascist Party. In 1936 conquered Ethiopia and in 1939 annexed Albania. When the Allies invaded Italy, Mussolini was ousted by Badoglio and imprisoned, but German parachutists rescued him. In April 1945 he was captured by Italian Partisans and shot.

Mussolini   Patton

Patton, George (1885-1945), American general, led the United States troops in the invasion of North Africa and commanded the U.S. 7th Army in the invasion of Sicily. In 1944, at the head of the 3rd Army, advanced rapidly across France, through South-West Germany and into Czechoslovakia and Austria.

Paulus, Friedrich (1890-1957), German field marshal and tank specialist, ended the Battle of Stalingrad when he surrendered the German 6th Army to the Russians on January 31, 1943.

Pétain, Henri Philippe (1856-1951), Marshal of France. Became a French national hero for his part in the Battle of Verdun in World War One. As Minister for War in 1934, he sponsored the ill-fated Maginot Line. After the fall of France in 1940, Pétain made terms with the Germans. At the end of the war he was found guilty of treason and sentenced to death. The sentence was commuted to life imprisonment.

Rommel, Erwin (1891-1944), German field marshal nicknamed the "Desert Fox", commanded the Afrika Korps in the Western Desert. After Alamein, he was given a command in France. He took part in a plot to kill Hitler with a bomb in 1944. The plot failed and Rommel poisoned himself.

Roosevelt, Franklin Delano (1884-1945), President of the United States 1933-45. Assisted the Allies by supplying war material before Pearl Harbour. Took part in two historic meetings with Churchill and Stalin at Teheran and Yalta. Died three weeks before the Germans surrendered.

Rommel   Roosevelt

Runstedt, Karl Rudolf von (1875-1953), German field-marshal. Directed the *blitzkrieg* in Poland 1939 and France 1940. In 1942 appointed to a command stretching from Holland to Italy—including the "Atlantic Wall." After the Allied invasion of Europe in 1944, he led the German armies in the Battle of the Bulge. Captured by the Americans, he was too ill to be tried but spent some time as a prisoner in Britain.

Stalin, Josef (1879-1953), Soviet Union head of state. Josef Dzhugashvili changed his name to Stalin and rose to be head of the Communist Party in the U.S.S.R. dealing ruthlessly with all rivals. He joined the Allies when Germany invaded Russia. Was the sole survivor of the "Big Three" at the Potsdam Conference in 1945, Truman replacing Roosevelt, Attlee replacing Churchill. From this time on, the gap between the West and Russia widened.

Stalin   Truman

Stauffenburg, Count Berthold von (1907-44), a colonel on the German General Staff in 1944 he was one of the ringleaders in the plot to assassinate Hitler on July 20. He put the bomb in position but, by chance, Hitler moved to a place where he escaped serious injury. Stauffenburg was shot next day.

Tito, Marshal (1893-   ), Yugoslav Partisan leader born Josip Broz. Learned Communism as a P.o.W in Russia in World War One and took part in the 1917 Russian Revolution. After the fall of Yugoslavia in 1941, Tito organized guerilla bands to harry the Axis forces. In 1945 Tito became Yugoslavia's first Communist Prime Minister.

Tojo, Hideki (1885-1948), Japanese soldier. Rose to be Minister of War in 1940-41 and from 1941 premier and dictator of Japan. He resigned in 1944. On arrest by the victorious Allies, he tried to commit suicide but failed and was put to death as a war criminal.

Truman, Harry S. (1884-1972), President of the United States 1945-53, took over as president when Roosevelt died. While in Potsdam in July 1945 for the conference with Stalin and Attlee, he heard that scientists in the United States had successfully tested an atomic bomb and he took the decision to use this new weapon against Japan. After the war, he guaranteed American aid to any free nation resisting Communist propaganda or sabotage.

Wavell, Archibald, 1st Earl (1883-1950), British field marshal. Made C.-in-C. British Forces Middle East in 1939, Wavell defeated the Italians in East Africa and in 1940-41 conducted a brilliantly successful campaign in the Western Desert. Was C.-in-C. India 1941-43, Viceroy of India 1943-47.

Yamashita, Tomoyuki (1885-1946), Japanese general, commander of the forces which overran Singapore in 1942. Afterwards took over in the Philippines and captured Bataan and Corregidor. He was captured and hanged for war crimes.

Zhukov, Grigori Konstantinovich (1896-   ), Russian marshal. Lifted the siege of Moscow in December 1941 and in February 1943 counter-attacked from Stalingrad. As commander of the Russian 1st Army in 1944-45 he captured Warsaw and occupied Berlin. On May 8, 1945 he accepted the German surrender.

Poems and Songs of the War

△ **T. S. Eliot,** the British poet, essayist, and Nobel prizewinner, wrote *The Four Quartets* in 1943. It is one of his major works, and two stanzas are printed below.

The Four Quartets

The dove descending breaks the air
With flame of incandescent terror
Of which the tongues declare
The one discharge from sin and error.
The only hope, or else despair
   Lies in the choice of pyre or pyre—
   To be redeemed from fire by fire.

Who then devised the torment? Love.
Love is the unfamiliar Name
Behind the hands that wove
The intolerable shirt of flame
Which human power cannot remove.
   We only live, only suspire
   Consumed by either fire or fire.

T. S. Eliot (1943)

[*Collected Poems, 1902-1962,* Faber and Faber Ltd., London.]

The first World War produced songs which are still sung and poems which are still held in high regard. World War Two produced very little of either. At first sight, this seems strange, but there were reasons for it.

The songs of World War One reflected the real feelings of the men who sang them as they marched. The determined cheerfulness of Tommy Atkins was reflected in *Pack Up Your Troubles in your Old Kit-Bag,* his homesickness in *Keep the Home Fires Burning* and *It's a Long Way to Tipperary.* This was in the days before radio, when troops marched instead of riding in lorries.

Some of the songs of World War Two seem to have been written by men who knew nothing of soldiering or of the serviceman's outlook. Songs like *We're Going to Hang Out the Washing on the Siegfried Line* and patriotic songs like *This is Worth Fighting For* and *There'll Always be an England* were clearly written to keep up the public morale, and would soon have been forgotten but for constant plugging on the radio. Only two songs struck the right note: *Lili Marlene,* the song of Rommel's Afrika Korps which the British soldiers "captured", and *We'll Meet Again,* sung by Vera Lynn.

In 1914, Rupert Brooke could write "Now God be praised who matched us with His hour", because he was expressing the people's belief that the war was a crusade. Young men joined up in a spirit of exhilaration. Only later did poets like Siegfried Sassoon and Wilfred Owen say what the fighting men knew, that war was not a glorious adventure but a filthy business.

Few thought that war was glorious in 1939. It was a dirty job which had to be done, and the poetry of World War Two consists not of trumpet calls to glory, not even of mourning for human folly, but more of personal reflection. Poets like Alun Lewis, Roy Fuller, Robert Conquest, John Pudney and Alan Ross wrote of their friends and of their deaths, of their own moods and boredom in distant places. They were more cynical than their fathers, for they were serving and some of them were fighting not to lead mankind to a Golden Age but simply for survival.

So the poetry of this war does not speak of patriotism nor often of horror and despair. It speaks more intimately of the feelings of men in uniform; in songs to the women they loved, in tributes to friends, in laconic obituaries to the dead. It is quiet poetry in a minor key.

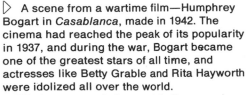

▷ A scene from a wartime film—Humphrey Bogart in *Casablanca,* made in 1942. The cinema had reached the peak of its popularity in 1937, and during the war, Bogart became one of the greatest stars of all time, and actresses like Betty Grable and Rita Hayworth were idolized all over the world.

Efforts were made to provide the armed forces with films for their entertainment wherever they were. A portable screen might be set up in the open air and a projector on the back of a lorry; after dark, a film would be screened with the audience sitting on the ground.

War Dead

With grey arm twisted over a green face
The dust of passing trucks swirls over him,
Lying by the roadside in his proper place,
For he has crossed the ultimate far view
That hides from us the valley of the dead.
He lies like used equipment thrown aside,
Of which our swift advance can take no heed,
Roses, triumphal cars—but this one died.

Once war memorials, pitiful attempt
In some vague way regretfully to atone
For those lost futures that the dead had dreamt,
Covered the land with their lamenting stone—
But in our hearts we bear a heavier load:
The bodies of the dead beside the road.

Gavin Ewart (1945)

[*The Terrible Rain: The War Poets 1939-1945*, Methuen 1966.]

△ **Gavin Ewart** was 23 and already a poet when war broke out: he writes of the dead with a kind of flat realism.

Poem

We're neither saint nor stoic,
Just craftsmen of the sky.
Our fighting's unheroic
And quietly we die.
We have no Heaven to buy with blood,
No Hero's world to give.
We do not seek to make man good;
Only let him live.

Geoffrey Richards

△ **A Spitfire pilot** sums up the modest outlook of the fighting man.

_____

▷ **Louis Simpson** was an American infantryman who could not bring himself to write about the war until it was over. He writes to remember the truth of what it felt like to be a soldier under fire.

The Battle

Helmet and rifle, pack and overcoat
Marched through a forest. Somewhere up ahead
Guns thudded. Like the circle of a throat
The night on every side was turning red.

They halted and they dug. They sank like moles
Into the clammy earth between the trees.
And soon the sentries, standing in their holes,
Felt the first snow. Their feet began to freeze.

At dawn the first shell landed with a crack.
Then shells and bullets swept the icy woods.
This lasted many days. The snow was black
The corpses stiffened in their scarlet hoods.

Most clearly of that battle I remember
The tiredness of eyes, how hands looked thin
Around a cigarette, and the bright ember
Would pulse with all the life there was within.

Louis Simpson

[*The Poetry of War 1939-45*. Alan Ross Ltd., 1965.]

Graves: El Alamein

Live and let live
No matter how it ended
These lose and, under the sky,
Lie befriended.

For foes forgive,
No matter how they hated,
By life so sold and by
Death mated.

John Pudney

[From *Collected Poems* of John Pudney, Putnam]

Plotting World War Two History (1)

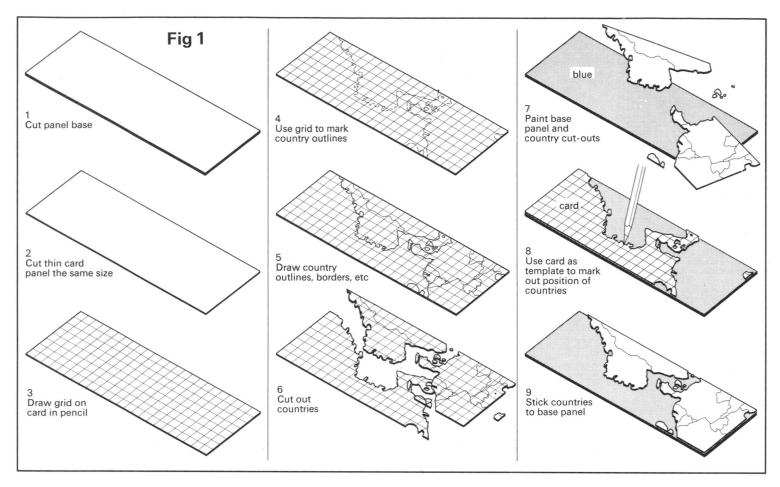

Fig 1

1 Cut panel base

2 Cut thin card panel the same size

3 Draw grid on card in pencil

4 Use grid to mark country outlines

5 Draw country outlines, borders, etc

6 Cut out countries

7 Paint base panel and country cut-outs

blue

card

8 Use card as template to mark out position of countries

9 Stick countries to base panel

The project on pages 58–61 is how to make a set of maps, drawn to scale, on which you can plot out all the battles, invasions, troop movements etc. of the war, either on your own or with a group. You may find that making the maps and following the war on them will help you to understand the events more clearly.

Making the Maps

First decide on the *size* of maps you are going to make. This really depends on the amount of space you have available to spread them out and work on them. Choose one size from the following:

size (i) for laying out on a table top. Here map 1 is made 12″ (300 mm.) deep by 4″ (100 mm.) wide.
size (ii) which is twice size (i), if you are going to work with your maps spread out on the floor, or possibly pinned to a wall.
size (iii) if you have a larger area to work with, such as a classroom.

You then need to cut out seven panels, one for each of the maps required, using the dimensions shown in the box below.

These panels can be cut from thick card, or even

rigid corrugated card for size (i). For the larger sizes it will be better if you use softboard, but card again will do. Hardboard is not suitable as it is too tough for pins to be easily pushed into it. Opposite are outline plans for seven maps. These are all drawn to scale, with a grid, enabling the outlines to be copied easily and quickly. The grid corresponds to the following dimensions:

size (i) $\frac{1}{2}$″ (12.5 mm.) squares
size (ii) 1″ (25 mm.) squares
size (iii) $1\frac{1}{2}$″ (40 mm.) squares

Stages in making a map are shown in Fig. 1, illustrating Map 1, but the stages are similar in each case, except for Map 5.

After the base panel has been cut out to the correct size, cut a second panel of the same size from *thin* card. On this draw out the grid squares, to the correct size as shown above.

Now refer to the key Map 1 opposite. Draw the outlines of the countries, and borders, following the points where they cross the grid on the key map. Each solid "block" representing a country or countries joined together is then cut out with scissors, or a modelling knife.

Before assembly, the base panel should be

painted, using poster colours or emulsion paints. The base panel should be painted blue (representing sea). The cut-out card pieces can be painted in different colours for each country—just as in a historical atlas, for example.

Take the piece of thin card which remains after you have cut out the "countries" and lay it over the map panel. Mark around the edges of the cut-outs with a pencil. These lines will serve as guides later on when you are gluing down the "countries" to the base panel.

You will now need to complete the details of your map. For example, the position of all the major cities in each country should be marked, and named, using an atlas for reference. Add any other geographical details you think are likely to be significant in war history. Some you will find mentioned in earlier pages of this book. Others you will have to discover through further reading. You can make the detailing of your map as elaborate, or as simple, as you like.

	Map 1	Map 2	Map 3	Map 4	Map 5	Map 6	Map 7
size (i)	12″ × 4″	12″ × 4″	12″ × 12″	12″ × 4″	24″ × 4″	12″ × 8″	18″ × 8″
	(300 × 100 mm.)	(300 × 100 mm.)	(300 × 300 mm.)	(300 × 100 mm.)	(600 × 100 mm.)	(300 × 200 mm.)	(450 × 200 mm.)
size (ii)	24″ × 8″	24″ × 8″	24″ × 24″	24″ × 8″	48″ × 8″	24″ × 16″	36″ × 16″
	(600 × 200 mm.)	(600 × 200 mm.)	(600 × 600 mm.)	(600 × 200 mm.)	(1200 × 200 mm.)	(600 × 400 mm.)	(900 × 400 mm.)
size (iii)	36″ × 12″	36″ × 12″	36″ × 36″	36″ × 12″	72″ × 12″	36″ × 24″	54″ × 24″
	(900 × 300 mm.)	(900 × 300 mm.)	(900 × 900 mm.)	(900 × 300 mm.)	(1800 × 300 mm.)	(900 × 600 mm.)	(1350 × 600 mm.)

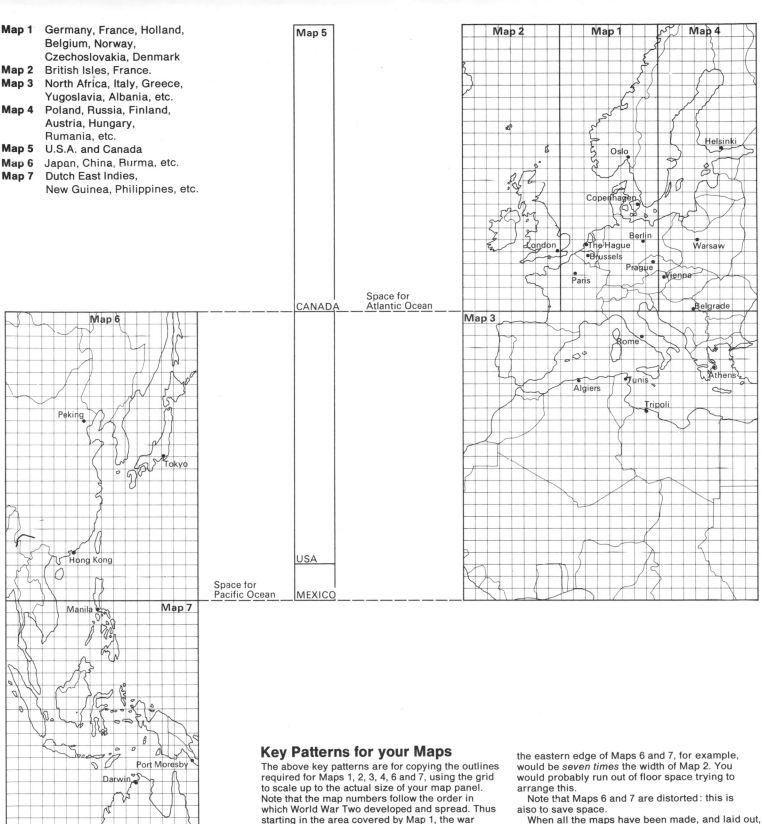

Map 1 Germany, France, Holland,
Belgium, Norway,
Czechoslovakia, Denmark
Map 2 British Isles, France.
Map 3 North Africa, Italy, Greece,
Yugoslavia, Albania, etc.
Map 4 Poland, Russia, Finland,
Austria, Hungary,
Rumania, etc.
Map 5 U.S.A. and Canada
Map 6 Japan, China, Burma, etc.
Map 7 Dutch East Indies,
New Guinea, Philippines, etc.

Key Patterns for your Maps

The above key patterns are for copying the outlines
required for Maps 1, 2, 3, 4, 6 and 7, using the grid
to scale up to the actual size of your map panel.
Note that the map numbers follow the order in
which World War Two developed and spread. Thus
starting in the area covered by Map 1, the war
spread into Map 2, then Map 3, and so on. As each
map is made, it is laid down in its correct position
with regard to the other map(s).

Map 5 is the exception. This covers Canada and
the United States. Since no military action took
place inside these countries during the war, the
whole area can be represented by a narrow strip,
to save space. Also to save space, it can be placed
fairly close to the maps in the 2-1-4-3 group—
"squeezing" the Atlantic into a channel. If you
have the space, of course, you can lay out Map 5 at
the proper scale distance from the western edge of
maps 2 and 3. This would be *five times* the width
of Map 2.

Maps 6 and 7 come later, and cover the war in
the Far East. Again the distance separating them
from America can be reduced to save space. Scale
spacing between the western coast of Map 5 and

the eastern edge of Maps 6 and 7, for example,
would be *seven times* the width of Map 2. You
would probably run out of floor space trying to
arrange this.

Note that Maps 6 and 7 are distorted: this is
also to save space.

When all the maps have been made, and laid out,
make sure that they line up correctly east-to-west.
America (Map 5) lines up "square" with the
Europe group. The bottom of Map 6 comes level
with the bottom of Map 5, with Map 7 underneath.
The complete history of World War Two can be
followed in detail by building up all the maps in
turn, plotting the course of military, aircraft and
naval activity on each as it developed. No area
covered remained static during the war years, so
each map is subject to continual change, indicated
by movement of symbols, etc.

If you have a camera—or can borrow one—
taking photographs of each map or group of maps
after each major change can provide a wonderful
record of the whole war. Check with an expert
photographer on the sort of lighting to use, and a
suitable exposure setting for your camera—or,
better still, get him to help you with your first shots.

Plotting World War Two History (2)

Symbols for Troops, Aircraft, etc.

Now make a collection of symbols to represent the troops, guns, tanks, aircraft, etc., of the various nations so that these can be positioned on your map to show the progress of the war in that area.

You can use glass-headed pins of a particular colour for the military forces of one particular country. The simplest type of symbol is a small paper flag mounted on such a pin. You can mark key drawings on the little flags. Some suggestions are shown in Fig. 2. These will not cover all your needs. You will have to think up other symbols as required.

Movement of aircraft is simple. You simply advance the aircraft symbol from its airfield position to the city or area being attacked. Troops, however, move on a broader front, occupying ground. You can show the extent of the advance by a line of pins (troop symbols), and then connect each pin with a length of coloured wool to show the area captured or occupied.

Fill in the area with appropriate colour as well, if the occupation looks like being permanent. (If one colour paint does not take well over the other, cover the area to be repainted with a cut-out pattern of plain paper first.)

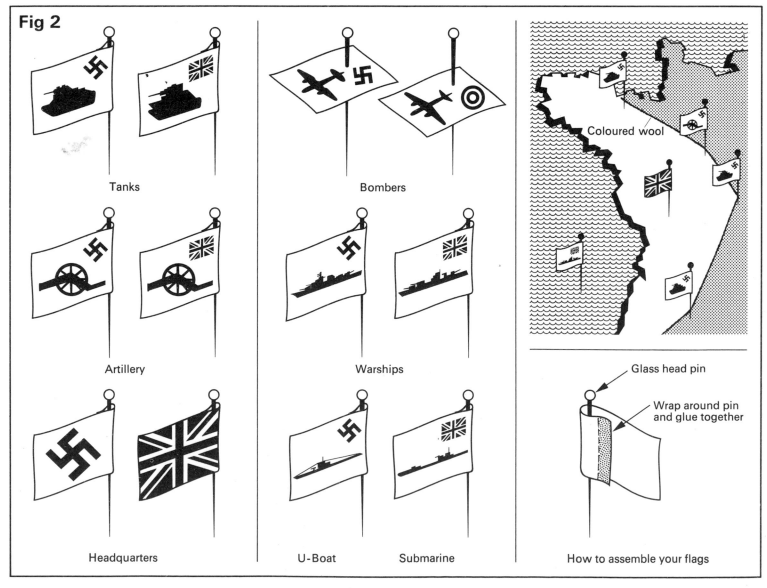

Fig 2

Tanks

Bombers

Coloured wool

Artillery

Warships

Glass head pin

Wrap around pin and glue together

Headquarters

U-Boat

Submarine

How to assemble your flags

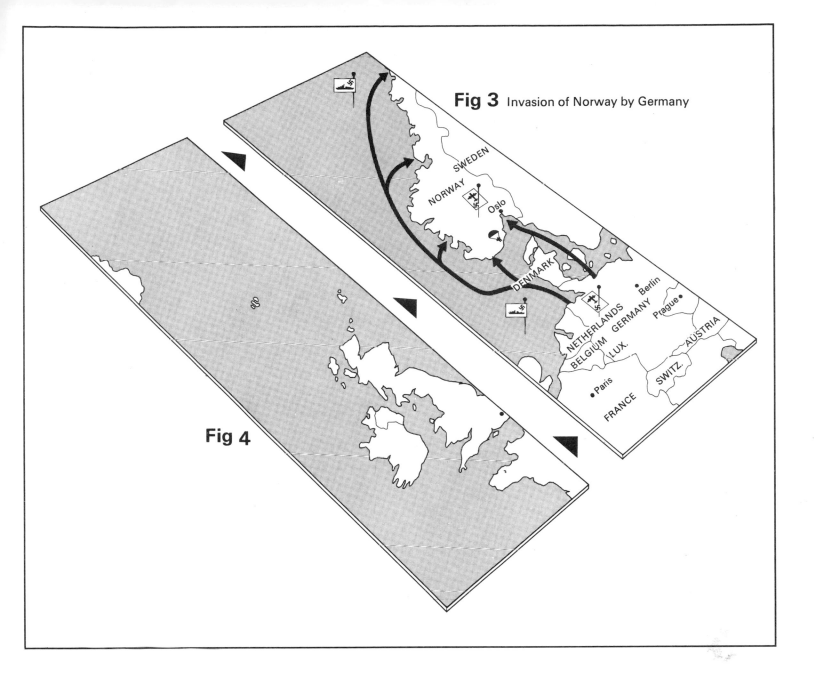

Fig 3 Invasion of Norway by Germany

Fig 4

Start with Map 1

Map 1 covers the Declaration of War and the War in the North, as described in the earlier pages of this book. This will give you enough information to plot the air attacks on the cities of the Netherlands, and the tank and troop movements into this country. Occupation by the German Army was rapid, so your map will settle down to a fairly static position after the first few movements. Fig. 3 will give you some idea of how this will look.

Look up other books on the early days of the war to find out what else happened after this. For example, there were aircraft "raids" from England dropping leaflets—plus real raids on a small scale. These make interesting plotting subjects.

The Norwegian area also offers interesting scope for further research. Consult the Reference Section of this book (p. 50-1) and see what else you can find to plot through further reading. The first significant naval actions occur in this area.

Follow with Map 2

Map 2 brings Britain into the picture—notably the Battle of Britain in the autumn of 1940 and the end of the "phoney war". Most of the major military operations involved bombing raids, which can be plotted individually.

Map 2 is made just like Map 1, with the same size of map panel and laid in position alongside Map 1 (see Fig. 4). There is a lot of scope here for plotting the position of fighter airfields in Britain; also the home ports and movements of the battleships and cruiser forces. Mark the ship names on the symbol flags.

Map 3

This map needs a larger panel—the same depth as the previous maps, but a width three times greater. This brings in the Balkans, the southern Mediterranean areas and North Africa.

Here are some highlights worth plotting: (you can discover others from further reading).

Italy invades Greece.
Germany invades Greece, Yugoslavia.
Battle of El Alamein.
Operation *Torch*.
Invasion of Sicily, Italy by Allies.

Map 4

Map 4 brings Russia into the war, with an unexpected invasion by Germany with whom they had a non-aggression pact. Here you can plot troop movements on a vast scale, and the final halting of the "invincible" German Army. Eastern Russia is not shown on Map 4, but you could make an extra map and fit it up against the others.

Here are some suggestions for major events to trace and plot:

Russia invades Finland.
Russian offensive against Germans.
Russians enter Poland, Rumania, Yugoslavia.
Russians reach Vienna.

Map 5

Map 5 is really for reference only, but if liked, you can use the space between Map 5 and the maps of Europe for plotting the Battle of the Atlantic: the years of the great convoys—and the near-disastrous losses inflicted by U-boats. Can you discover the turning point in the battle? Was it the fact that eventually air cover could be provided for convoys over the whole of the Atlantic route, with aircraft operating from bases in America and Britain?

Map 7

Map 7 brings in Australia, always under threat of Japanese invasion, but the Japanese advance finally stopped at—where? Mark it on the map and see how far south and east the Japanese reached.

Having set up Map 7, you will now have to return to Europe again—North Africa, Italy and eventually the D-day landings, with the big air raids on German cities and the final encirclement of Germany.

In the Pacific (Maps 6 and 7) you can plot:

British withdrawal in Malaya, Burma.
Japanese invade Burma, New Guinea.
Battle of Coral Sea.
U.S. troops land on Guadalcanal.
Battle of Leyte Gulf.
Atomic bombing of Hiroshima, Nagasaki.

Index

Further Reading

Available in the United States and Canada:

AMBROSE, STEPHEN E. *The Supreme Commander: The War Years of General Dwight D. Eisenhower*. Doubleday 1970.

BEACH, EDWARD L. *Submarine!* Holt 1952.

BRICKHILL, PAUL. *Great Escape*. Norton 1950.

CHURCHILL, SIR WINSTON S. *The Second World War*. 6 volumes. Including *The Gathering Storm*. Houghton 1948. *Their Finest Hour*. Houghton 1949. *The Grand Alliance*. Houghton 1950. *The Hinge of Fate*. Houghton 1950. *Closing the Ring*. Houghton 1951. *Triumph and Tragedy*. Houghton 1953.

COLLIER, BASIL. *The Second World War: A Military History; From Munich to Hiroshima—In One Volume*. Morrow 1967.

DUPUY, TREVOR N. *The Military History of World War II*. 19 volumes. Watts 1962-1970.

HERSEY, JOHN. *Hiroshima*. Knopf 1946. *Into the Valley; A Skirmish of the Marines*. Knopf 1943.

HOWARTH, DAVID A. *D-Day, the Sixth of June, 1944*. McGraw 1959.

HOYT, EDWIN P. *How They Won the War in the Pacific: Nimitz and His Admirals*. Weybright 1970.

KEITH, AGNES NEWTON. *Three Came Home*. Little 1947.

LIDDELL HART, B. H. *History of the Second World War*. Putnam 1971.

LORD, WALTER. *Day of Infamy*. Holt 1957.

MONTAGU, EWEN. *The Man Who Never Was: A True Story of Counter-Espionage*. Rev. ed. Lippincott 1967.

MOSLEY, LEONARD. *On Borrowed Time; How World War II Began*. Random 1969.

PATTON, GEORGE S., JR. *War As I Knew It*. Houghton 1947.

SALISBURY, HARRISON E. *The 900 Days; The Seige of Leningrad*. Harper 1969.

SMITH, S. E. *The United States Navy in World War II*. Morrow 1966.

SULZBERGER, C. L. *The American Heritage Picture History of World War II*. Simon & Schuster 1966.

TOLAND, JOHN. *Battle: The Story of the Bulge*. Random 1959. *The Last Hundred Days*. Random 1966. *The Rising Sun; The Decline and Fall of the Japanese Empire, 1936-1945*. Random 1970.

WILLIAMS, ERIC. *The Wooden Horse*. Junior ed. Abelard 1958.

Available in Britain:

BAYNE-JARDINE, C. C. *World War Two*. Longmans 1968.

BRICKHILL, PAUL. *The Dam Busters*. Cadet edn. Evans 1963.

DUPUY, TREVOR N. *European Land Battles: 1939-1943. European Land Battles: 1944-1945*. Watts 1963. *Air War in the West: September 1939-May 1941. Air War in the West: June 1941-April 1945. Land Battles: North Africa, Sicily, Italy. Naval War in the West: the Raiders. Naval War in the West: the Wolf Packs*. Watts 1964. *Asiatic Land Battles: Allied Victories in China and Burma. Asiatic Land Battles: the Expansion of Japan in Asia. Asiatic Land Battles: Japanese Ambitions in the Pacific*. Watts 1965. *Air War in the Pacific: Air Power Leads the Way. Air War in the Pacific: Victory in the Air. Naval War in the Pacific: On to Tokyo. Naval War in the Pacific: The Rising Sun of Nippon*. Watts 1966. *European Resistance Movements. Asian and Axis Resistance Movements*. Watts 1970.

FARRAR-HOCKLEY, ANTHONY. *The War in the Desert*. Faber 1969.

FOX, EDWARD. *The Battle of Britain, August-September 1940*. Lutterworth Press 1969. *Desert Victory*. Lutterworth Press 1967.

HOBLEY, L. F. *The Second World War*. Blackie 1971.

McELWEE, WILLIAM. *The Battle of D-Day*. Faber 1965.

PEACOCK, ROY. *The Second World War*. Macmillan 1970.

SAVAGE, KATHERINE. *A State of War: Europe 1939-1945*. Blond Educational 1964. *The Story of the Second World War*. Oxford University Press 1957.

SCOTT-DANIELL, DAVID. *World War II*. Benn 1966.

SELLMAN, R. R. *The Second World War*. Methuen 1964.

SMITH, N. D. *The Battle of Britain*. Faber 1962.

WILLIAMS, ERIC. *The Wooden Horse*. Junior edn. Collins 1955.

Acknowledgements

We wish to thank the following individuals and organizations for their assistance and for making available material in their collections.

Key to picture positions:

(T) top (C) centre (L) left (B) bottom (R) right and combinations; for example: (TC) top centre.

Associated Press *p. 18-19(BC)*
Australian War Memorial *p. 42(CL)*
Central Press *p. 5(TR), 57*
Hulton Picture Library *p. 19(TL), 31(TR), 49(TR), 56(TL)*
Imperial War Museum *p. 10(BL), 11(TL), 12(TL), 17(T), 18(CL) (BL), 19(BR), 23(BR), 32-33(BC), 33(CL) (CR), 35(BR), 37(BL) (BR), 39(TR) (CR) (B), 41(CL), 43(TR), 45(CL), 47(CR), 52(BL)*
Keystone *p. 52(TL)*
Library of Congress *p. 27(B)*
Life © 1972 Time Inc. *p. 44(BL)*
National Archives *p. 46(TL)*
Novosti *p. 20(TL), 21(BR), 34(B), 36(TL) (BL), 44(TL)*
Plant News *p. 5(TL)*
Popper, Paul *p. 30(BL), 31(TL)*
Rijksinstitut voor Oorlogsdocumentaire *p. 31(BR)*
Science Museum, London *p. 11(BR)*
Search *p. 21(TL), 37(CL)*
Signal *p. 16-17(BC)*
Südd-Verlag *p. 39(TL)*
Tritschler-Opera Mundi *p. 36(BR)*
Ullstein *p. 6(BL), 7(CL), 31(TC), 45(TL), 50(BL)*
U.S. Air Force *p. 12-13(BC), 47(T)*
U.S. Army Dept. *p. 40(CL), 41(BR), 45(TR)*
U.S. Marine Corps. *p. 43(TR)*
U.S. Navy *p. 41(TL) (CL), 46(CL)*

Artists and photographers

Amsden, Deirdre *p. 28(L), 29(BR), 30(TL)*
Batchelor, John *p. 8-9(B), 10(TR) (CR) (BR), 13(BR), 17(BR), 20(BL), 21(BL), 24-25(C), 27(T), 30-31(BC), 32(BL), 33(T), 35(T), 37(T), 38(B), 38-39(C), 40(BR), 41(BL), 42-43(BC), 43(C), 45(BR), 46-47(BC)*
Butler, Liam *p. 13(CR)*
Harrison, Chris *p. 24(B), 25(TL) (B), 35(BL)*
Taylor, Peter *p. 6(R), 9(TL), 15(CR), 16(BL), 21(TR), 26(B), 40(T), 43(TL), 44-45(B), 48(R), 49(B), 53(TR) (B), 58-61*

Project author

R. H. Warring

If we have unwittingly infringed copyright in any picture or photograph reproduced in this publication, we tender our sincere apologies and will be glad of the opportunity, upon being satisfied as to the owner's title, to pay an appropriate fee as if we had been able to obtain prior permission.